Travel and Intercultural Communication

To Ingrid

INTRODUCTION

Dear Readers,

Let us take you on a journey—wrap up warm though—we are going north!

It all began with a dear friend. We, the editors of these proceedings, inherited an impressive collection of travelogues about travelling in the North from our much-missed colleague Ingrid Neumann when she passed away in 2011. Ingrid gave it to us in the hope that we would make something out of the multifaceted stories ranging from the early 1700s to today. However, the books gathered more and more dust in our offices until one day a young colleague, Oana Cogeanu, asked us whether we would be willing to work on a project about travel literature together with Romania. This gave us the opportunity to go both east and north in a project together with Alexandru Ioan Cuza University of Iaşi, and to write about our own material.[1]

These are the proceedings of "Going North: An Interdisciplinary Conference on Travel and Intercultural Communication" held in Halden, Norway, in 2016. We live in a global network where spatial, linguistic and cultural mobility is reshaping our identities. This mobility is unprecedented in its scope, and caused by a multitude of reasons from pure leisurely travel to desperate flight. The "Going North" conference explored mobility from an interdisciplinary perspective, addressing the role of travel—past and present—and intercultural communication connected to travel.

In the following you will travel through texts focusing on going north from several geographical points of departure, there will be different genres to roam between and you will come across intercultural aspects such as issues of identity, othering, the crossing of borders, and, certainly, cultural perceptions of the North. If you have packed your bags and put on

---

[1] The project, ENTICE, was financed by EEA-grants and was a joint venture of Alexandru Ioan Cuza University of Iaşi, Romania and Østfold University College, Norway. We were given the opportunity to co-host one conference in Iaşi, Romania, "Going East" (June 2015), and one in Halden, Norway, "Going North" (February 2016). In addition, we were sponsored by Østfold University College.

your scarves and mittens, we are now ready to introduce you to both itinerary and guides.

The first part of our journey deals with *encountering the Other and the possibility of crossing borders*. First we meet Kathryn Walchester from Liverpool John Moores University in the United Kingdom. She focuses on the representation of servants in nineteenth-century travel writing about journeys north by British female writers, and argues that these paid companions occupied a pivotal role in intercultural negotiations between the British employer/traveller and the alterity of the North. Arranging essential practical details such as food, accommodation and clothing, servants, either British servants brought on the journey or locals hired on arrival, had a much closer experience of the "foreign" than their employers. Addressing texts by Mary Wollstonecraft, *Letters Written During a Short Residence in Sweden, Norway and Denmark* (1796), Lady Di Beauclerk, *A Summer and Winter in Norway* (1868), and Mrs. Aubrey Le Blond, *Mountaineering in the Land of the Midnight Sun* (1908), Kathryn explores the various roles played by these working travellers and how they played a significant textual as well as practical role on the journey. Moreover, in addressing the role and representation of this group of people, she addresses the pervasive issue of mobility and class in relation to the typology of the "traveller".

Saying goodbye to Kathryn we go for a drive through Sweden with Eva Lambertsson Björk and Jutta Eschenbach from Østfold University College, Norway. They guide us together with Wilson MacArthur who in the summer of 1946 travelled with his wife in their sturdy Standard Twelve, "the Black Beetle", from Great Britain through Sweden. They have resumed their nomadic life style from before the Second World War, and are "footloose and free", with the aim to come as close as possible to Sweden and its people. Eva and Jutta discuss the author-narrator's response to otherness and difference in his encounters with the Swedes, as reported in the travelogue *Auto Nomad in Sweden* (1948). In their analysis they draw on Syed Manzurul Islam's concepts of the sedentary and nomadic travellers, the former with a focus on difference, the latter on "becoming-other". The travelogue is characterized by two kinds of discourse. The more descriptive parts convey information about the Swedes from an essentialist cultural perspective, focusing on differences. The more personal passages report on the author-narrator's attempts to change perspectives, to "become-other". However, the question remains to what extent a self-declared nomad actually can cross the line and "become-other", as he is constantly on the road. Eva and Jutta discuss a traveller who aims to come close to the "other" through openness and understanding. However, he is only marginally successful in his nomadic endeavor.

After this we visit the animal kingdom by travelling north together with Melanie Duckworth, Østfold University College, Norway. She claims that nature is often figured as the opposite of culture. In other ways, however, cultures define themselves by the way they interact with the natural world. Melanie discusses the work of Kathleen Jamie, who in her journeys to Scandinavia and northern Scotland seeks a conversation with the natural world, but in the process encounters and engages in conversations between cultures, such as that between English, Scottish, Danish and Swedish conservators working together in Norway to repair whale skeletons from the Nineteenth Century. Whales have prompted many journeys to the North, both in the past for the purpose of whaling, and in the present for the purposes of tourism and conservation. Melanie investigates how, in Jamie's writing, whales and their physical remains participate in intercultural communication as symbols of northernness and the natural world. Ultimately, Jamie seeks to look beyond this to the whales themselves, creatures who make their own journeys and with whom, if we are lucky, we may travel north together.

Our next stop is in Russia together with Maria Selezneva, University of Exeter, the United Kingdom. She tells us about her work based on travel guides about Russia and their English translations. The concepts, which characterize Russia as a civilization of the North, are studied in translated texts. There is a special focus on translations of different types of northern weather, clothes and food. These phenomena are common in Russian culture, but they are new for those who have never experienced a northern way of life. Cultural translators strive to make travel guides as understandable for readers as possible. This strategy, a so-called domesticating strategy, means that translators and travellers transfer cultural meanings through a comparison with the culture of "home". This strategy is a major step towards the decision-making of untranslatability in intercultural translation. Maria's aim is to show that a domesticating strategy not only leaves cultural differences unchanged, but also makes them more comprehensible for the readers of travel guides about a remote and unusual northern culture of Russia.

Leaving Russia behind, we gather up our bags and move into the second part of the journey that is about *perceptions of the North and issues of identity and ways of thinking*. Our first guide in this part is Janicke Stensvaag Kaasa, University of Oslo, Norway. She takes us to the "New" Canadian North. She explores the idea of the mysterious in postwar representations of the Canadian North, with particular emphasis on Pierre

Berton's critically acclaimed and best-selling travel book *The Mysterious North* (1956). Despite its concern with economic and strategic developments in the postwar North, the region in Berton's text remains a spectral, mythical and enigmatic land—"a country of unanswered questions"—which tends towards the imaginary. By keeping the North in the realm of the mysterious Berton draws on familiar ideas of an unfamiliar region, which contributed to the book's success and to the consolidation of Berton as a northern voice.

Leaving Canada we then travel together with "Sikorski's Tourists" from Poland to Britain in the company of Joanna Witkowska, University of Szczecin, Poland. On September 1st 1939, Germany's attack on Poland marked the beginning of World War II. After over a month of fighting the Poles lost, but were determined to continue their struggle for independence. The collapse of France in June 1940 made Britain "the Last Island of Hope" and thus going north became the call of the day for the Polish military. German propaganda disparagingly called them "Sikorski's tourists". For many Polish combatants Britain became the final destination and wartime home as they fought under British command. Consequently, they became involuntary travellers to and then in the country which most of them had not visited before. After the war, many of them published their recollections in which they described their intercultural encounters with the British other. Joanna presents the nature of these Polish-British relations by focusing on the Polish perception of the geographical and metaphorical North. Referring to their published reminiscences as the primary sources she argues that although these Poles travelled north in their capacity of soldiers, their journey turned out to be also the journey of self-rediscovery.

After this, as strange as it may sound, we take a trip south to envision the North, guided by Karen Patrick Knutsen, Østfold University College, Norway. Her paper concerns a transitory stage in the poetry of Irish writer Seamus Heaney (1939-2013)—the collection *North* (1975). During the troubles in Northern Ireland, Heaney, an Irish Catholic and prominent intellectual, was under public pressure to take a political stance in his writing by either supporting or condemning the republican cause. He refused, insisting that poetry should not be forced to play a part in political struggles. Consequently, he left his post at Queen's University in Belfast in 1972, and moved south to become a citizen of the Irish Republic. *North* was the first volume of poetry he published after his move. Henry Hart sums up *North* as follows: "Heaney wrestles with the call to become more politically engaged and ultimately resists it for the safer, more private ardours of poetry" (1992, 76). Although Hart's judgement is partially true,

Part 1:

Encountering the Other—
Crossing Borders?

CHAPTER ONE

EMPLOYMENT, MOBILITY AND INTERCULTURAL COMMUNICATION IN BRITISH TRAVELOGUES FROM THE LONG NINETEENTH CENTURY

KATHRYN WALCHESTER

In Letter One of Mary Wollstonecraft's 1796 *Letters from a Short Residence in Sweden, Norway, and Denmark,* Wollstonecraft describes the effect of her maid's concerns, as the small party, consisting of Wollstonecraft, her baby Fanny Imlay and her maid Marguerite, prepare to go ashore on the Swedish coast near to Gothenburg.

> The day was fine; and I enjoyed the water till, approaching the little island, poor Marguerite, whose timidity always acts as a feeler before her adventuring spirit, began to wonder at our not seeing any inhabitants. I did not listen to her. (Wollstonecraft 1796, 3–4)

This extract is taken from Wollstonecraft's famous journey of 1795, which was made to try to recover some of her partner Gilbert Imlay's shipping fortune. Despite her own insecurities about his fidelity whilst she was away, she presents herself in this section as strident, confident, and very different to her maid. Wollstonecraft undercuts her account of Marguerite's concerns with the retort "I did not listen to her". Marguerite had been hired in Paris by Wollstonecraft in 1794 and stayed with her and the child for the rest of Wollstonecraft's life (Ferguson and Todd 1984, 114). Remarkably in the extract Marguerite is depicted as being more sensitive to the environment than Wollstonecraft, that most famous of Romantic women travellers. Wollstonecraft ignores Marguerite's reading of their surroundings at first, dismissing her fears as part of her characteristic "timidity". However, in the following lines Wollstonecraft admits her own concerns.

> But when, on landing, the same silence prevailed, I caught the alarm which
> was not lessened by the sight of two old men, whom we forced out of their
> wretched hut. (Wollstonecraft, 4)

Wollstonecraft, her maid and baby are preparing to go ashore in Norway
for the first time after travelling from France. Marguerite's understanding
of the situation proves infectious and Wollstonecraft concedes that she too
is afraid of making contact with the Norwegian natives on the shore. The
two women decide to return to their boat, having learned that there is no
possibility of the old men taking them to Gothenburg. Their second
attempt at putting ashore is similarly fraught with fear for Marguerite.
Wollstonecraft describes how the pilot boats are under the direction of a
lieutenant, who can speak English, and who approaches their ship with the
intention of collecting the women himself. Wollstonecraft again outlines
the initial differences in her own and her maid's response. She writes:

> To save the sailors any further toil, I had my baggage instantly removed
> into his boat; for, as he could speak English, a previous parley was not
> necessary; though Marguerite's respect for me could hardly keep her from
> expressing the fear, strongly marked on her countenance, which my putting
> ourselves into the power of a strange man excited. (Wollstonecraft, 7)

Once again Wollstonecraft describes Marguerite as more fearful of the
foreign environment and the people who live there than she is. Marguerite
cannot help but show her emotions. Wollstonecraft's actions have, from
the maid's perspective, put them both in danger. In textual terms
Marguerite is set up as a foil to Wollstonecraft, reinforcing the status
of the author-traveller. By representing herself as more confident,
Wollstonecraft's narrative persona is bolstered as the "expert traveller" in
contrast to Marguerite, who is, in the narrator's view, too wary.

This paper focuses on a group of people, like Marguerite, whose
travels have largely been regarded only in terms of their association with
more famous, often leisured and higher status writers and travellers. In the
paper, I consider how working travellers feature in accounts of travels to
Norway from the long nineteenth-century, beginning with *Letters from a
Short Residence in Sweden, Norway, and Denmark* by Mary
Wollstonecraft, published in 1796, *A Summer and Winter in Norway* by
Lady Diana Beauclerk, published in 1868, and finally *Mountaineering in
the Land of the Midnight Sun* by Mrs. Aubrey le Blond (1908). Within this
focus I discuss the representation of several paid travelling companions
whose roles and statuses are very different from each other: Marguerite,
Wollstonecraft's maid is also nurse to Wollstonecraft's child; in Lady Di
Beauclerk's text Teresina is a lady's maid to both Beauclerk and her

mother; and in the final text Mrs. Aubrey le Blond discusses both her mountaineering guides, Joseph Imboden and his son Emil, as well as a Norwegian woman, Hildur, who is employed to cook and organise the details of their camp. All of these servants, in their various roles, encountered the "other" of Norway differently to their employers, often acting as an intermediary between the employer-traveller and the foreign.

James Clifford identified the problematic issue of the status of the mobility of servants and slaves in the late 1990s, when he asked,

> Does the labor [sic] of these people count as "travel"? Clearly, a comparative cultural studies account would want to include them and their specific cosmopolitan viewpoints. But in order to do so, it would have to thoroughly transform travel as a discourse and genre. (Clifford 1997, 34)

Clifford highlighted the way in which accounts by servants and slaves have often been elided from travel writing, noting that, "their experiences, the cross-cultural links they made, their different access to the societies visited—such encounters seldom find serious representation in the literature of travel" (Ibid., 33). By focusing on the representations of these working travellers, I want to interrogate, as Clifford asserts, "their experiences, the cross-cultural links they made, their *different* access to the societies visited" (Ibid.). For although Marguerite, in the extract with which I began, is represented as hesitant of her encounter with Norwegians, it was certainly the case that servants were required to have considerable contact with people in foreign destinations in order to organise the practicalities of the journey; and in this case, Marguerite was subsequently left with baby Fanny, for almost six weeks in Gothenburg at the home of Gilbert Imlay's Swedish agent, Elias Backman (Todd 2000, 325, 339). The "cross-cultural" links and different access to the society visited, in this case Norway, form a part of what Ingrid Piller has identified as under a wide definition of "intercultural communication"; those situations "where culture is made relevant" through "discursive constructions" (Piller 2011, 8). The "discursive constructions" evident in travel writing comprise of both the verbal interactions which pre-figure the travelogue, and the textual rendering of these encounters. The presence of the servant-traveller adds a dimension to the conventional binary of "traveller" and "travellee", with the servant as intermediary or occasional representative of the native culture (Pratt 1992, 7). As such the servant-traveller's role is that of an "agent of transculturation", using Sebastian Jobs and Gesa Mackenthum's term, a "border-crosser, mediator [or] go-between", negotiating between cultures and acting out the "multilaterality of cultural interaction" (Jobs and Mackenthum 2013, 9).

The Textual Representation of Servants

The trope of the invisible servant has become a commonplace in understandings of nineteenth-century society; one which scholarship in architecture, art and fiction have frequently reinforced (Trodd 1989, 8; Hill 1996; Gerard 1994). More recently, scholars such as Julie Nash, in her account of the works of Gaskell and Edgeworth, have argued that in the eighteenth and nineteenth centuries servants were "expected to be socially invisible" (Nash 2007, 11; Lethbridge 2013, 19). In contrast, studies by Bruce Robbins and others since the 1990s began to question the extent to which servants were erased from view in fictional texts (Robbins 1993; Fernandez 2010). The eighteenth-century novel in particular is marked by the ubiquitous presence of servants, and often ones who travel. Thus the eponymous hero of Tobias Smollett's *Humphry Clinker* is a man-servant, albeit the long-lost son of Matthew Bramble. Likewise, in Laurence Sterne's *A Sentimental Journey*, Yorick's long-suffering French servant La Fleur forms a major part in the anecdotes related by the narrator. Earlier in the century there are protagonists such as Moll Flanders (Defoe 1722), Richardson's Pamela (1740), and Fielding's Tom Jones (1749). This presence in fiction continued into the nineteenth century, with central characters such as Jane Eyre and Nelly Dean from texts by Charlotte and Emily Brontë, and travelling side-kicks such as Passepartout in Verne's *Around the World in Eighty Days* (1873).

Servants take a much smaller part in the travelogues of the nineteenth century than in their fictional precursors however. This paper goes some way to considering the reasons for that lack of presence, and also in excavating how, when servants *are* described, their representation indicates their role in both the practical and textual production of journeys; that is, how, where, and why servants were included in travelogues. Certainly, as many studies have asserted since, servants were integral to the fictions, lives and, in this case, the journeys of the middle and upper-classes of the eighteenth and nineteenth centuries. In a concurrent focus on the material and the textual production of travel, this paper addresses social historian Caroline Steedman's appeal and challenge to Bruce Robbins, that the consideration of the roles of workers such as these should necessarily acknowledge that, "Servants were not [merely] signposts left at random in the no-man's land between what could and could not be represented" (Steedman 2007, 356) and to consider where they do appear in the text and what such a consideration might contribute to our understanding of intercultural communication in nineteenth-century travel to Norway.

Since James Clifford's question about the inclusion of journeys of work or compulsion into a wider understanding of travel, calls for the journeys of servants and others who participated in non-elite, non-leisured travel to be acknowledged has been repeated in the work of Tim Youngs, John Hutnyk and more recently in relation specifically to working women travellers by Jennifer Bernhardt Steadman (Youngs 2002; Hutnyk in Clark 1999, 48; Steadman 2007). In his account of The Grand Tour of Southern Europe for example, James Buzard acknowledges that alongside the aristocratic, leisured journey of the Grand Tour, "many other kinds of journeys, undertaken by many sorts of people for many purposes, were going on" but notes that they "must be consigned to the margins of the still central tale of the Grand Tour" (James Buzard in Hulme and Youngs 2002, 38).[1] There are many challenges to such an extension of the field of travel writing studies however, not least that many servants did not write their own accounts of their journeys, and if they did, they were rarely retained, let alone published. In spite of such challenges, it is clear that servants' contributions to the history of mobility in the eighteenth and nineteenth centuries are essential to our understanding of how journeys took place and what their various travellers experienced during the travels.

Servants enabled the journeys of their leisured employers and, in their mobility, encountered many more vicissitudes than their employers as they attempted to work in unfamiliar environments and often with a lack of facilities for them to fulfil their duties effectively. In his account of servants accompanying Grand Tourists, Christopher Hibbert notes that "the choice of these [servants] was also important, since much was required of them" (1997, 23). Servants had little control over the choice of destination or modes of transport. Their employers decided where the party would travel, and in the cases cited the employers were relatively young or inexperienced travellers; none of them having visited Scandinavia before. There was an expectation that servants would have to work harder when travelling than at home in order to maintain domestic standards, especially on camping expeditions such as Le Blond's or when residing in rural farmhouses as in Beauclerk's trip. On their return to Christiania for example Beauclerk notes the extra work her maid Teresina is required to do to repair the damage to their clothes caused by their

---

[1] In their accounts of Grand Tour travel both Jeremy Black and Christopher Hibbert note the ubiquity of servants. See Hibbert, *The Grand Tour* (London: Methuen, 1987), p. 23, and Jeremy Black, *Italy and the Grand Tour* (New Haven and London: Yale University Press, 2004), p. 6, for example.

journey.[2] She writes, "Teresina, with extra aid called in, set to work to repair the injuries that travels by land and sea had inflicted on our wardrobes" (Beauclerk 1868, 104). Servants brought from Britain on journeys around Scandinavia were most often domestic or personal servants, whereas those intermediaries hired in Norway helped with the displacement of the traveller as guides, cooks and porters, for example *or*, more often, they could act as cultural mediators, occupying roles such as translators, interpreters, tour guides and negotiators.

Thus accounts of the travels of working travellers should not be consigned to the margins or continued to be rendered invisible. Rather, an analysis of the representation of and by servants extends the typology of the traveller, enriches our understandings of intercultural exchange, and contributes to a more comprehensive understanding of "leisure travel" in the nineteenth century. My approach towards these texts, drawing from Said's reformulation of the musical term, is a contrapuntal reading. According to Said, to read contrapuntally involves a focus on the sub-dominant which re-emphasises and provides a new equilibrium between the various voices. In this study the sub-dominant voice is that of the servant, and by focusing on this aspect in particular, it is hoped that understandings of so-called "leisure travel" will be rendered more resonant (Said 2000, 186).

The Practical Roles and Textual Functions of the Travelling Servant

The servants' presence in these travel texts was central, not only to the practical aspect of the journeys therefore, but also to the composition of the travelogues. References to, and descriptions of, servants constitute the narratorial identity of the employer-narrator and have a strategic role in the construction of narrative shape. In the later stages of the journey, overland through Denmark, Wollstonecraft describes her maid's response to their travels and reflects on their different attitudes.

> We travelled the remainder of the day, and the following night, in company with the same party, the german [sic] gentleman whom I have mentioned, his friend, and servant: the meetings, at the posthouses, were pleasant to me, who usually hear nothing but strange tongues around me. Marguerite and the child often fell asleep; and when they were awake, I might still reckon myself alone, as our train of thoughts had nothing in common,

---

[2] In this paper, place names are taken as per the original text, thus in Beauclerk's text Christiania is used rather than Oslo.

Marguerite, it is true, was much amused by the *costume* of the women; particularly the *panier* which adorned both their heads and tails; and with great glee recounted to me the stories she had treasured up for her family, when once more within the barriers of dear Paris; not forgetting, with that arch, agreeable vanity peculiar to the french [sic], which they exhibit whilst half ridiculing it, to remind me of the importance she should assume when she informed her friends of all the journeys by sea and land— shewing the pieces of money she had collected, and stammering out a few foreign phrases, which she repeated in a true Parisian accent. Happy thoughtlessness; ay, and enviable harmless vanity, which thus produced a *gaité du Coeur* worth all my philosophy. (Wollstonecraft, 234—235)

Although Wollstonecraft finishes this long extract by equating Marguerite's attitude to travelling with her own, it is implicit in the language of the previous comparison that we are to regard the value which Marguerite has gained from her travels as inferior to Wollstonecraft's own insights. Referring to her maid's stories repeatedly as "vanity", which will be told to raise her status amongst her friends, and the extent of Marguerite's acquisition of Scandinavian languages as "stammering out a few foreign phrases", Wollstonecraft's comments seem dismissive of the results of her servant's encounter with the "other". In fact, such is Wollstonecraft's measure of the difference between their attitudes that Wollstonecraft notes that she might "still reckon [herself] alone". Wollstonecraft's detailed account of the servant's reactions to the journey reinforces the position and status of herself as narrator-traveller. Thus in contrast to Marguerite's superficial "vanities", Wollstonecraft counterpoints herself as "philosophical traveller".

The account of Marguerite, here, fulfils another narrative function. The gentle mocking of Marguerite's contrasting attitudes and reactions to travel is textually expedient; during a long coach journey, when, as Wollstonecraft notes, "there was little in the prospects to awaken curiosity" and "the heaths were dreary and had none of the wild charms of those of Sweden and Norway to cheat time" (Wollstonecraft, 237—238). Thus the journey is dull at this point, there is little in the scenery to excite Wollstonecraft's interest, and the turn to focus on Marguerite's reactions serves to lighten the mood and interrupt the tedium of the description of overland travel. This technique is one used in other travelogues from the period, which describe journeys to Norway and across other European countries. Thus in early nineteenth-century travel accounts of Italy, the long journey south between Florence and Rome, is repeatedly punctuated by accounts of Gothic encounters with servants in strange inns, for example.[3]

Lady Diana de Vere Beauclerk's journey, which took place in 1867 and which forms the basis of *A Summer and Winter in Norway*, likewise featured a long overland journey into the interior of Norway north of Christiania up to Aak, a distance of more than 400 kilometres. Lady Di, as she fashioned herself, was twenty-six when she travelled to Norway with her mother and their French maid Teresina. She was the daughter of the ninth Duke of St. Albans and went on to marry Sir John Walter Huddleston in 1871. Beauclerk and her party's mode of travel to Norway is indicative of the changes in travel to Norway from the middle of the century and is more in-keeping with that of middle-class tourists; the women travelled from London to Christiania by the North Star steamer, setting off on 25th July 1867. After a stay in Christiania, Beauclerk, her maid and mother made the journey north-west by train and then by driving individually in carioles, Norwegian two-wheeled carriages. They did not rush; as Beauclerk writes, "Fifty miles a day is quite enough for ladies who travel for pleasure, and who enjoy stopping for an hour in the middle of the day for the purposes of refreshment" (Beauclerk, 32). Teresina, Beauclerk's French lady's maid, who appears very little in the text as a whole, becomes a focus on this long carriage journey north. Beauclerk describes how,

> In fact, Teresina had never driven before, and evidently her notion of driving had more of progress than of prudence, with limited notions of the perils of obstruction. The result was, that, applying her whip and neglecting the reins, she ran into my mother's cariole, and a serious smash was nearly the consequence. However, all was soon righted and; the accident taught Teresina a lesson not easily forgotten; and, I am bound to add, she soon became a most experienced Jehu. (Beauclerk, 28)

The description of Teresina as a Jehu is a reference to one of the Kings of Israel, who was a notoriously fast and reckless driver. Thus Teresina not having had the experience of carriage driving in England is represented in comic terms and on the journey, references to Teresina's accidents occur several times. The effect of these anecdotes is to lighten the monotony of the description of the long overland journey. Once the rural landscape has been described in the travelogue, other material must be added to give the impression of the passing of time, without losing the interest of the reader.

---

[3] See Walchester, *'Our Own Fair Italy': Nineteenth-Century Women's Travel Writing and Italy: 1800—1844* (Oxford and Bern: Peter Lang, 2005), p. 117.

Thus Teresina's misadventures provide entertaining interludes to the account of the long journey.

On the return journey, Teresina's reckless driving is again a focus, and here another textual function of the anecdotes is illustrated; that of indicating a contrast between the employer-narrator and the servant-traveller. Beauclerk describes the party driving finally into Christiania,

> For some reason which was never clear to my mind, whereas hitherto I had led the way all through our journey, my mother would drive first into the city, and, for reasons best known to herself, went rather fast. Teresina likewise, evidently anxious to prove to the world the experience she had gained in driving, pressed closely on me, so that between the pace my mother went and Teresina's anxiety to be close up, I fully expected a smash; but the Fates were propitious, and we finally drove in all possible state and grandeur to the Scandinavian Hotel. (Beauclerk, 97)

Compounded with the interest these anecdotes about Teresina's misadventures when driving provide to the long journey sections of the text, they also provide a counterpoint to the persona of the traveller-author. Where Beauclerk is a skilful driver, "prudently" allowing Teresina to pass in her cariole, to avoid yet another accident in Dovre; Teresina is reckless and gets caught up in the moment as when she races Beauclerk's mother into the capital.

A further point of contrast established by Beauclerk between herself and her maid is Teresina's apparent passivity when faced with the challenges of travel to and in Norway. When struck with terrible sea-sickness for example Beauclerk describes her maid being "carried to her own berth" by the stewardess and notes that she was "seen no more till we landed at Christiansand" (Beauclerk, 11). Later in the text the account of a moment of drama allows Beauclerk to illustrate the contrast between her own reactions and those of Teresina's more starkly. The party stay for several days at Nystuen despite the advice of their local guide, Carlsen. She describes how,

> Here, in spite of our courier, we remained several days, sledging and walking over the frozen river, possibly to show our courage, which, however, one day received a shock which I, for one, did not easily get over. When half across, one morning, the ice suddenly cracked with an alarming noise. The guide called to me to run for my life, which I did, leaving my French maid, who had fallen down from fright, a helpless looking bundle on the ice. In due time, the danger, which, I believe, had more of noise than peril, disappeared; the guide returned, picked up Teresina, and we got safely back. (Beauclerk, 91—92)

Teresina's reaction contrasts to that of the narrator. Becoming helpless and inanimate, a "helpless-looking bundle", Teresina requires assistance from the guide to cross the ice, where Beauclerk does not. This scene is reminiscent of the representation of Teresina suffering from sea-sickness and being carried to a cabin. In both cases Beauclerk depicts herself as self-reliant. The employer is active, running across the frozen river successfully, albeit having been frightened herself. The "shock" noted by the narrator draws attention away from the difficult situation of the travelling servant and the fact that she must follow her employer even if the situation is dangerous.

The principal reason that servants are often silenced or reduced to comic roles in travelogues therefore centres on the construction of the author as "expert traveller". Where in a novel the author can distance him- or herself from the narrative persona, travelogues are, as Mary Baine Cambell argues, "a kind of witness; . . . generically aimed at the truth" (1988, 2—3). Thus in the construction of herself as narrator-traveller, the author often distinguishes herself from other travellers, and their actions. One of the most frequently employed strategies to achieve this juxtaposition between servant-traveller and employer-traveller is the representation of the servant as the unwilling or unhappy traveller; or as in Wollstonecraft's depiction of Marguerite, appreciating very different aspects of the journey than themselves. In *A Summer and Winter in Norway* Beauclerk marks her status as "expert traveller" through such a depiction of Teresina. Where Beauclerk relishes her stay in the interior of Norway, away from the social pleasures of the capital, Teresina is relieved to be returning to Oslo after their extended stay in the countryside. Beauclerk notes that,

> Teresina was delighted to return. That she recounted her adventures to an admiring audience, I have no doubt; but in sober truth, very few ladies'-maids would have been so good-tempered, made themselves so useful, or fallen so readily into the changes and chances of our travels as did Teresina. (Beauclerk, 100)

Alongside the praise of her servant, Beauclerk indicates the difference in their reactions when returning to Christiania. This is made more obvious when considered in contrast with Beauclerk's description of their final day driving the carioles.

> Doing anything for the last time, knowing it is to be so, is always sad, and I cannot agree in thinking a pleasure well over is a victory gained—at least we did not think so when we tucked ourselves into our respective carrioles [sic] to make our last day's journey to Christiania, and give up that

> delightful Bohemian existence, the hardships of which exist only in the
> minds of those who have never travelled to Norway. (Beauclerk, 96)

Beauclerk's appraisal of the "delightful Bohemian existence" was
evidently one not shared by her maid, most likely due to the change of
environment and lack of facilities for her to fulfil her duties effectively. As
in Wollstonecraft's account of Marguerite, Beauclerk emphasises that
Teresina will recount "her adventures to an admiring audience",
underlining the maid's communication of her experiences of Norwegian
life to her friends back home, and the subsequent rise in status this affords
her (Beauclerk, 100). In this regard both Wollstonecraft and Beauclerk
seem to belittle their maids' experiences of travelling and patronise their
actions of enjoying the attention their experiences allow. It is clear in both
texts that the authors regard travelling as significant to their own status
and development and yet they do not celebrate the achievements of their
servants. The root of this contradiction emerges from the centrality of the
understanding of independence in the history of travel. As Clifford asserts,

> A host of servants, helpers, companions, guides, and bearers have been
> excluded from the role of proper travellers because of their race and class,
> and because theirs seemed to be a dependent status in relation to the
> supposed independence of the individualist, bourgeois voyager. (1997, 33)

Teresina and Marguerite are regarded according to this construction as
"dependent", in that they are not orchestrating their own journeys, but
rather accompanying their employers. Thus as in Clifford's appraisal they
are excluded from the status of "proper traveller". However, when their
contribution to the practicalities of the journey is considered, this
dependence is called into question; just as the apparent independence of
their employers, who are reliant on significant amounts of support, is
suspect in Clifford's comments.

Beauclerk's text was one of many travelogues about Norway by the
end of the 1860s, and she uses several strategies to signal the difference
between her text and those by other women writers. First, she emphasizes
that unlike many other travellers she stayed in Norway through the winter,
albeit in the environs of Christiania; and secondly she makes much of her
and her mother as "unprotected females", making overt references to
Emily Lowe's notorious travelogue *Unprotected Females in Norway* from
1857. Beauclerk's assertion that they are "three unprotected females . . .
landed on a foreign shore" was not in fact true, and Teresina, as we have
seen from the earlier reference to their guide, was not their only servant
(Beauclerk, 18). In Chapter Three she notes,

I had forgotten to mention that we had engaged a courier, and picked him up at Christiansand. Carlsen was his name, and he proved himself, during the whole of our residence in Norway, an invaluable and faithful servant. (Beauclerk, 18)

Speaking the native language Carlsen provided the party with food at inns, made reservations and organized horses. He took on the role of what was referred to on the southern tour as the *valet-de-place*.

In contrast to travels to France and Italy, journeys to Norway more often necessitated the hire of a local interpreter or guide because of difficulties with the language. Independent traveller, Emily Lowe, the self-professed "unprotected female", ridiculed the use of couriers, interpreters and guides. Lowe writes,

Tolks, or interpreters, a mild sort of courier, were never heard of some years ago, and are most absurd appendages in a country where travelers must either sit in the kitchen or in their own bedrooms. (Lowe 1857, 85)

Lowe's assertion is that because of the lack of high class destinations in Norway, British travellers do not need to converse much with the natives and therefore do not require an interpreter. Lowe spends "more than a week at Christiania on purpose; not to master [the language] grammatically as an English savant was trying, but to pick up the principal words, and try to catch how the natives strung them together" (Lowe 1857, 72). More often however, the avoidance of hiring a *tolk* or local courier did not seem to be a decision based on the traveller's wish to relate more closely with the local people in Norway. John George Holloway, in his 1853 travelogue *A Month in Norway*, had noted,

I see no necessity for *men* to take with them an interpreter or courier, if they choose to take a little extra trouble of informing themselves before starting of a few essential particulars. Where ladies are of the party, an intelligent and experienced *tolk* (interpreter) will be found a great comfort, if not exactly a necessity. (Holloway 1853, 43)

Making oneself independent of local people, including guides, interpreters and couriers, often seemed to be the aim in attempts by the traveller at learning the language or geography of the country; that and reducing the cost of the trip. Of course, if the employer-traveller hired a local guide, an intermediary such as Carlsen, there may have been less need for interaction between any British servant and the Norwegian people with whom the party stayed.

Hiring a local servant, such as Carlsen, in Beauclerk's case, or Hildur, the cook in Le Blond's text, adds another dimension to the intercultural communication between the traveller-employer and the native population. The local servant acts as an intermediary to the native culture and can introduce the employer-traveller to new approaches to everyday life, which seems to have been the case with Mrs. Aubrey Le Blond.

Mrs. Aubrey Le Blond, or Elizabeth Hawkins-Whitshed as she was before her marriage, travelled to Norway first in 1898 with two Swiss guides, Joseph Imboden and his younger son Emil, in order to climb on the Lyngen Peninsula in the far north of Norway. Le Blond had climbed extensively in the Alps, often with Joseph and his elder son who had been killed in a climbing accident some years earlier. She was the first British woman acknowledged to have climbed in Norway, and was the first president of the Lyceum Club, later to become the Ladies' Alpine Club (Thompson 2010, 74; Williams 1973, 62—65). Her 1908 publication *Mountaineering in the Land of the Midnight Sun* draws together five years' of climbing anecdotes from Norway and several camping and fishing holidays with her husband. It is during one of these camping trips that Le Blond and her husband hire Hildur, a young woman from the far north of the country, who teaches them something about how to drink coffee,

> Six summers of such coffee [writes Le Blond] as drank daily in those regions have utterly ruined my liking for coffee elsewhere. And the strange thing about it is, that it is made in the simplest possible manner. A hundred times have I seen Hildur make the coffee, and made it myself in the same way, and always has it turned out perfection. Yet, when I have returned home and entreated my cook to follow on the same lines, the coffee has been undrinkable, as it invariably is, to my mind all over France and Switzerland. (Le Blond 1908, 127)

Hildur introduces Le Blond to a new way of making and drinking coffee, which Le Blond takes up, but its cultural movement ceases there, Le Blond cannot translate the method across to the servants in England. Le Blond introduces Hildur in an early chapter describing her impressions of the Norwegians. It is Hildur's presence in their camp and Le Blond's relationship with her which form the basis of Le Blond's generalizations about Norwegians. She writes:

> We were often surprised, when talking to Norwegians in a humble station, to find how easily they met us on ground familiar to both. We noticed this specially when, during our three last seasons in the North, we had a servant. (Le Blond, 61)

Le Blond's detailed account of Hildur, which follows this extract, is unusual for texts about Norway during this period. There are few accounts of Norwegian individuals in British travelogues from the nineteenth century, especially about a servant. The scant reference to Carlsen in Beauclerk's text is much more typical. However, Le Blond's use of Hildur as an exemplar for her class is not valid; she is not "in a humble station". As Le Blond goes on to indicate, Hildur is from a relatively affluent background:

> Our maid, Hildur, was a person of surprising versatility. She came from Bødø [sic], just on the verge of the Arctic Circle, and we heard of her through a servant of a fishing party with whom we travelled down the coast. Hildur, with the enterprise of her countryfolk, was quite ready to embark on a rough life in camp with people she had never seen. I believe she came at first from sheer curiosity, for her father was well-to-do, and she expressed herself as amply satisfied with the very modest wages she asked. She spoke not one word of English, but she had supplied herself with a Norwegian-English dictionary, and so ready was she in jumping to correct conclusions, that in quite a short time she had taught herself a fair amount of our language, and had imparted to us a goodly number of words and phrases of her own. (Le Blond, 61)

The intercultural communication works both ways here, Hildur, it seems, does not really need to work for the English couple, indicated by the modest wages she asks and her well-to-do father, but goes on the camping expedition with them, as Le Blond asserts, out of "sheer curiosity". Hildur uses the opportunity to learn some English and to teach Le Blond and her husband some Norwegian. Le Blond's account of Hildur highlights the agency of the servant. Their actions in taking on positions which enabled them to travel and gain experience of foreigners or foreign places are an important and perhaps overlooked aspect in the travels of those who were not travelling for leisure.

Le Blond refers to Hildur only once more, very briefly, in a chapter which details the way in which Le Blond and her husband set up camp. Their mode of residing in Norway is set out as different to other British visitors, and emphasizes their intention to get away from "the beaten track" and live a "simple life", ostensibly without interacting with others, particularly in hotels and on public transport. She describes how,

> During three more summers my husband and I, with our native maiden Hildur to cook for us, had an excellent time camping by those northern fjords and lakes . . . We set out determined on the simple life, and we certainly had it in all its simplicity. For where we went there we might fish

as we chose, shoot where we chose, and camp where we chose, and none
except an occasional Lapp or two honoured us with a visit. (Le Blond, 219)

Thus Hildur facilitates Le Blond's withdrawal from other Norwegians, and
also other tourists. Although she is cited as an example of the native
people and associated with the party's "simple life" in camp, it is clear that
Hildur is adopted as a trusted intermediary because of her respectable
social status and interest in communicating in English with Le Blond and
her husband. This is more apparent when Le Blond writes of the relief
they felt at not being disturbed by native people, other than the "occasional
Lapp", who are not described. In textual terms, the description of Hildur
has several important functions. Firstly, it acts to dilute and act as a break
in the many climbing anecdotes, and moreover, facilitates the textual
move into ethnographic observations in this section of the travelogue.
After the long account in praise of Hildur, Le Blond offers observations
more generally about Norwegian women, writing, "the women of Norway
struck me, on the whole, as singularly independent and capable" (Le
Blond, 61).

Despite le Blond's account of enjoyment of being off the beaten track
of the tourist routes, it is clear that she is dependent on Hildur and, when
climbing, on her Swiss guides Joseph and Emil Imboden, in order to
sustain this. In the mountaineering camps, it is Imboden and his son's
responsibility to carry out the majority of chores or tasks which involve
interaction with the Norwegian villagers. In a striking example when the
party is at Jaegervand, Imboden and his son are required to walk six miles
[about ten kilometers] to the village because Le Blond must get a letter to
the post. They cannot go by boat as a storm has washed their boat away
from its mooring and Le Blond does not walk with them because the walk
is too arduous, involving fording a river. Thus she is left alone in the camp
and begins to re-erect the tents after the storm and make a fire. Of her
solitude, she notes:

> So for the first time in my life I was left absolutely alone, miles from any
> other human being—quite, entirely alone! No one can picture a safer
> country than I was in. Still the experience of complete solitude, especially
> to a woman, is strange, and in my case was accentuated by the knowledge
> that I was in a place which it was not easy to get out of. (Le Blond, 110)

Apart from the fact that she has not been left alone before—at this point
she is at least forty years old—it is surprising that Le Blond seems
unnerved by being on her own in the relatively innocuous setting of the
riverside camp, especially when she has climbed mountains and

emphasized her courage at other points in the text. This incongruity illustrates the dependency with which Le Blond regards her guides and their centrality to her climbing successes. It is perhaps their comprehension of the significance of their role which prompts their return to the camp sooner than expected. She writes of how,

> As I reflected on our quaint existence and leisurely prepared to retire that evening I heard a distant call, and hastening to the back of the hut I presently saw my two guides striding down towards me, their pockets bulging with the incoming mail. They had determined, if at all possible, to return to me that night, and had gallantly forded rivers and plodded through bogs in order to do so. The villagers had entreated them to wait till next day, when they could return by boat; but they put the temptation aside, and insisted on setting out for a repetition of as unpleasant a walk as it is possible to imagine. (Le Blond, 114)

Le Blond's relief at seeing Imboden and his son returning to the camp is clear. Their interaction with the local people is evident; they arrive with pockets bulging with communication from home but also have been urged to wait until morning before returning to Le Blond in order to make their journey more easily. As well as her relief, Le Blond's pleasure at their return also centres on guides' loyalty and sense of duty towards her, ignoring local advice and their own hardship. The description of the guides as "gallant" indicates a sense of chivalry and their positions, not as servants, but men of a high social station. The absence of the guides allows a moment of adventure in the text, as the protagonist is alone in the camp; and breaks up the discussion of the various climbs they have achieved. It indicates her dependence on the guides and furthermore it indicates the role of the guides as intermediaries between the high-status Englishwoman and the Norwegian villagers.

As the examples from Beauclerk and Wollstonecraft have shown, the main fault of the servants is shown to be their lack of enjoyment of the experience of travelling, or at least their appreciation of what is perceived as the wrong sort of pleasures. And this feature, in turn, helps to project the author-traveller as an expert in comparison. Le Blond likewise outlines this view of the qualities of a guide in her opening chapters. She writes:

> It is essential to carefully choose the guides with a view to their travelling in countries new to them. Some guides become homesick and miserable directly they leave their native land. Others are not quick in adapting themselves to what I may call unconventional forms of mountaineering, particularly when wine is not obtainable. Others could hardly be brought into Norwegian hotels and houses on the same footing as their masters, and

no other footing is possible in a country where none travel with personal servants. (Le Blond, 21)

Le Blond follows this by noting that her guide, Imboden, "was the ideal travelling guide". She notes that "he and his son have been happy and contented, and have made friends with all classes" (Le Blond, 21). Imboden's success, for Le Blond, seems to be his adaptability, his ability to fit in with changes in circumstance and situations, particularly in relation to class. However, the central reason that Le Blond is able to portray Imboden as such a successful and admirable traveller and climber, is perhaps her gender. Where other female travellers were one of many, and needed to present themselves as different and more adept than their female servants, Le Blond's explicit claim at the novelty of her text is that she is the first woman to have climbed so extensively in Norway at this time. She notes in the preface, "In the following pages I hope to take lovers of mountains up a number of peaks that were till then untrodden" (Le Blond, 10). Thus, Imboden's expertise poses no threat to the projection of the authorial voice as expert-traveller in this case—instead Le Blond sets herself up in contrast to the tourist—as an adventurer.

In his article "Partners: Guides and Sherpas in the Alps and Himalayas, 1850s—1950s", Peter H. Hansen cites Alfred Wills, from his 1856 book, *Wanderings Among the High Alps*. Wills asserts that,

> A good guide is generally a very intelligent man . . . with a great love of nature and adventure, often, with a considerable amount of acquired information, and with manners more like those of a gentleman than are to be found amongst men of any other class, in the same rank of society. The guide acts [as] a sort of personal servant, almost a valet. (Wills 1856, 330)

Although Wills asserts the similarities between the mountaineering guide and the servant, it is clear from both Wills' account and from Le Blond's text that expectations are different for the guide, socially and in terms of their knowledge and experience. Such nuances draw attention to the differences in the representation of and the travelling experiences of servants, which require much more attention from the field of travel writing studies if we are to excavate more representatively the full range of travel. Hansen's main point in citing Wills is to indicate the range of roles carried out solely by the guide; of which one of the most important is that of cultural intermediary. Hansen notes that "Guides served as intermediaries with other communities . . . The guide also performed the role of porter and interpreter" (Hansen 1999, 214). Imboden's skills, his adaptability and his ability to communicate with a range of people, are particularly significant by the time of the publication of Le Blond's text. She asserts that by 1908, Norway is "a country where none travel with personal servants" (Le Blond, 21). Changes to Norway's travel infrastructure and the fact that it became a more affordable destination meant that a greater number of middle-class travellers visited Norway without domestic servants and instead relied on the services provided by hotels and couriers.

Conclusions

Le Blond's assertion that, "The last important duty of a guide is to *know* the way; while one of his first duties is to find it", is helpful in drawing together the functions, both textual and practical, of the servant-traveller and in articulating the significance of their role (Le Blond, 19). Le Blond's assertion indicates the centrality of the servant-traveller to the journey; finding the way, whilst the author-narrator follows. The quotation draws attention to the extent to which paid intermediaries were relied upon and expected to develop skills and knowledge, often through communication with locals, which they might not have had before travelling. The quotation also indicates the agency of the servant-traveller, that, rather than being passive companions on the journey, intermediaries were required to take the initiative, make connections with their employers, and local people and their ways of living, in order to facilitate and make possible these journeys.

References

Beauclerk de Vere, Lady Diana. 1868. *A Summer and Winter in Norway*. London: John Murray.
Burrows, Stuart. 2008. "The Place of the Servant in the Scale". *Nineteenth-Century Literature*, Vol: 63, No. 1, 73—103.
Campbell, Mary Baine. 1988. *The Witness and the other World. Exotic European Travel Writing. 400—1600*. Ithaca, New York: Cornell University Press.
Chamberlain, Erin Dee. 2007. *Servants, Space, and the Face of Class in Victorian Fiction* [unpublished PhD thesis]; Purdue University Graduate School.
Clarke, Steve, ed. 1999. *Travel Writing and Empire: Postcolonial Theory in Transit*. London: ZED books.
Clifford, James. 1997. *Routes, Travel and Translation in the Late Twentieth Century*. Cambridge, Mass.: Harvard University Press.

Gerard, Jessica. 1994. *Country House Life: Family and Servants 1815—1914*. New York: Wiley.

Ferguson, Moira, and Janet Todd. 1984. *Mary Wollstonecraft.* Woodbridge, CT: Twayne Publishers.

Fernandez, Jean. 2010. *Victorian Servants, Class and the Politics of Literacy.* London: Routledge.

Hansen, Peter H. 1999. "Partners: Guides and Sherpas in the Alps and Himalayas, 1850s—1950s". In *Voyages and Visions; Towards a Cultural History of Travel*, edited by Jás Elsner and Joan-Pau Rubiés, 210—231. London: Reaktion Books.

—. 2004. "E. A. F. Le Blond". Oxford Dictionary of National Biography. Oxford and New York, accessed October 31, 2013, http://www.oxforddnb.com/view/article/52565

Hibbert, Christopher. 1987. *The Grand Tour.* London: Methuen.

Hill, Bridget. 1996. *Servants: English Domestics in the Eighteenth Century.* Oxford and New York: Oxford University Press.

Holloway, George. 1853. *A Month in Norway.* London: John Murray.

Hulme, Peter and Tim Youngs, eds. 2002. *The Cambridge Companion to Travel Writing.* Cambridge: Cambridge University Press.

Jobs, Sebastian and Gesa Mackenthun. 2013. *Agents of Transculturation: Border Crossers, Mediators, Go-Betweens.* Münster and New York: Waxmann.

Le Blond, Mrs. Aubrey. 1908. *Mountaineering in the Land of the Midnight Sun.* London: T. Fisher Unwin.

Lethbridge, Lucy. 2013. *Servants: A Downstairs History of Britain from the Nineteenth Century to Modern Times.* New York: Norton.

Lowe, Emily. 1857. *Unprotected Females in Norway; or, The Pleasantest Way of Travelling There Passing through Denmark and Sweden, with Scandinavian Sketches from Nature.* London: Routledge.

Nash, Julie. 2007. *Servants and Paternalism in the Works of Maria Edgeworth and Elizabeth Gaskell.* Aldershot: Ashgate.

Piller, Ingrid. 2011. *Intercultural Communication: A Critical Introduction.* Edinburgh: Edinburgh University Press.

Pratt, Mary Louise. 1992. *Imperial Eyes: Travel Writing and Transculturation.* New York: Routledge.

Rigg, J.M. 2004. "Huddleston, Sir John Walter (1815—1900)" rev. Eric Metcalfe, *Oxford Dictionary of National Biography*, Oxford University Press. Online edition, May 2008, accessed April 16, 2013, http://www.oxforddnb.com/view/article/14027

Robbins, Bruce. 1993. *The Servant's Hand; English Fiction from Below.* Durham and London: Duke University Press.

Said, Edward. 2000. *Reflections on Exile and other Essays.* Cambridge, Mass.: Harvard University Press.

Steadman, Jennifer Bernhart. 2007. *Traveling Economies: American Women's Travel Writing.* Ohio: Ohio State University Press.

Steedman, Carolyn. 2009. *Labours Lost; Domestic Service and the Making of Modern England.* Cambridge: Cambridge University Press.

Thompson, Simon. 2010. *Unjustifiable Risk? The Story of British Climbing.* Cumbria: Cicerone.

Todd, Janet. 2000. *Mary Wollstonecraft; A Revolutionary Life.* New York: Columbia University Press.

Trodd, Anthea. 1989. *Domestic Crime in the Victorian Novel.* New York: St. Martin's Press.

Walchester, Kathryn. 2005. *'Our Own Fair Italy': Nineteenth-Century Women's Travel Writing and Italy. 1800—1844.* Oxford and Bern: Peter Lang.

Williams, Cicely. 1973. *Women on the Rope: The Feminine Share of Mountain Adventure.* London: George Allen and sons.

Wills, Alfred. 1856. *Wanderings Among the High Alps.* London: Bentley.

Wollstonecraft, Mary. 1796. *Letters Written During a Short Residence in Sweden, Norway and Denmark.* London: J. Johnson.

CHAPTER TWO

A BEETLE ON THE LOOSE—
WILSON MACARTHUR:
AN AUTO NOMAD IN POSTWAR SWEDEN

EVA LAMBERTSSON BJÖRK
AND JUTTA ESCHENBACH

Introduction

Travelling may involve a radical change of self, provided one is open enough and willing enough to let it do so. However, it may also be only transport from one place to another without any significant change of self. In the travelogue *Auto Nomad in Sweden* (1948)[1] by Wilson MacArthur, the author-narrator's goal is a change of self. In what follows we discuss his text in the light of this goal.

Auto Nomad in Sweden is the record of the author-narrator's first post-war trip abroad. It is the first of a series of books in which he labels himself an auto nomad (*Auto Nomad in Sweden* 1948, *Auto Nomad in Barbary* 1950, *Auto Nomad through Africa* 1951, and *Auto Nomad in Spain* 1953). *Auto Nomad in Sweden* covers going north from Gothenburg on the southwest-coast of Sweden to Kiruna far above the polar circle, and back again to Gothenburg—from 13 July to 16 September 1946 (Pier 1946, 1). The author-narrator hints at being commissioned to produce this travelogue. When asked about how long his trip will last, the question is avoided, but he comments "Secretly, we knew the answer: until the cash that Mr Dalton allowed us to take was finished" (AN 3). Further, he liaises with the Swedish Institute, established in 1945 to promote Sweden abroad.

---

[1] Macarthur Wilson, *Auto Nomad in Sweden* (London: Cassell & Co. Ltd, 1948); all subsequent text references will be cited parenthetically in the text as AN.

Auto Nomad in Sweden intrigued us. Our point of departure is the self-proclaimed status of the author-narrator as a travelling nomad, with an underlying implication of openness of mind and willingness to change perspectives. How does this proclamation tally with what is reported in his text? Is the author-narrator a nomadic traveller?

We draw mainly on Syed Manzurul Islam's concepts of the sedentary and nomadic traveller (Islam 1996).Travelling is obviously about moving to other places and about encountering differences. The way in which these differences are negotiated depends on whether one is a sedentary or a nomadic traveller.

Sedentary travellers merely move from one point to another to register differences:

> It seems that the movement of sedentary travel is driven by the need to secure a vantage point from which to carry out a representation of difference . . . sedentary travellers, burdened as they are by the need to establish essential difference . . . and to capture otherness in knowledge, obsessively bring into existence a rigid boundary which separates them from the other. (Islam 1996, viii)

Sedentary travellers produce knowledge about other places and people from an ethnocentric perspective. They focus on differences between themselves and others, thereby adopting an essentialist approach to culture, in which culture is seen as homogeneous. Through this "discourse of difference" (Ibid., 62) sedentary travellers establish boundaries. They move from place to place in space, but without responding to the others in a way that allows them to be changed themselves. They experience other places and people without, in the wording of Islam, "becoming-other" (Ibid., vii), without "crossing lines" (Ibid., 2).

Nomadic travellers, in contrast, are transformed by the encounter with the others: "Nomadic travel is to do with encounters with otherness that fracture both a boundary and an apparatus of representation: It is a performative enactment of becoming-other" (Ibid., vii). Nomadic travellers do not have the need to establish boundaries, rather their movements are about crossing lines to "become-other". We interpret "becoming-other" as being transformed through meeting people with other cultural backgrounds. To us it indicates the changing of perspectives: looking at things from the positions of the people one meets on one's journey. It indicates that the traveller and the others have established a "common discourse" (Islam 2014, 213). In contrast, sedentary travellers lack the openness necessary for transformation. They map what they see and focus on differences in a process of othering. "Othering", to us, implies a process where one identifies and addresses the differences between oneself and those of other cultural origins, without necessarily judging the other as inferior.

In our examination of the travelogue of a self-proclaimed nomad, we have developed two broad research questions:

1. What is the open road to the author-narrator?
2. To what extent does the open road lead to a change of the author-narrator's self?

Before taking a closer look at the open road that stretches out in front of Wilson MacArthur, let us introduce him. He was born in 1903 in Ayrshire, Scotland. During the 1930s he worked as fiction editor for the *Daily Mail* and the *Evening News.* During the Second World War he served in the British Navy with a number of books about the Royal Navy as a result. In the 1950s he settled down on his farm in Africa. However, he continued to travel extensively throughout his life. He died in 1981, probably in Richmond, South-Africa (http:// www.ayrshirehistory.org.uk/ postings1/macarthur.htm). MacArthur wrote a number of short stories and adventure novels, many of them set in exotic surroundings. In addition he wrote numerous travel books, and travelling seems indeed to have been both his passion and his main occupation. He travelled in Europe, in Africa and in America. MacArthur and his South-African wife Joan were travelling in Africa when the Second World War broke out. They managed to get back to Britain, but obviously could not travel extensively until the war had ended.

The Open Road

Already in the title the author-narrator establishes his identity by labelling himself an auto nomad. The term nomad has connotations of mobility, of wandering and of roaming far and wide, while the term auto refers to both autonomy and to the chosen means of transportation, his journey by car. The combination of the two terms serves to reinforce an image of an independent traveller.

How then does the author-narrator understand the concept of traveller? Let us take a closer look at what the introduction to his travelogue reveals. The author-narrator assumes a voice of authority as he shares his philosophy of how to travel with the reader, and concludes that it is best to travel by foot:

> It teaches you to discard the superfluous, to be happy with few possessions, and to rely upon yourself. It teaches you humility, and it gives you pride . . .

> there is no other way of coming to know a country and its people so
> intimately, so sympathetically; and no way that brings so many little daily
> adventures crowding upon each other's heels. I have walked many times.
> (AN ix)

This credo makes it clear that a traveller on foot by necessity has to focus
on what is essential, it is impossible to carry many possessions. Travelling
by foot also entails independence and a large measure of self-reliance.
Further, in teaching humility it offers the possibility of learning to know
one's innermost qualities, both strengths and weaknesses. It means to take
leave of one's known surroundings and exchange them for the unknown
where unforeseen things happen constantly. This, the author-narrator
argues, is the best way to get to know a country and its inhabitants. His
choice of the words "intimately" and "sympathetically" suggests that his
aim is to become so close to the people he meets, that he will be able to
see the world from their perspectives, something that necessitates crossing
lines. In this way the author-narrator underlines the nomadic aspect of his
identity, quite in line with Islam's concept of the nomadic traveller.

However, travel by foot has the great disadvantage that it takes time,
and distances are limited. Other solutions, the author-narrator continues,
may involve trains or buses. However, such means of transportation,
democratic as they may be, "cater for the big battalions; [and] despise the
individual" (AN ix). There are no possibilities for openness and
spontaneity since public transportation companies do not "wish to pander
to the whims of the moment" (AN ix), nor are there any possibilities for
the unexpected and unusual event, as public transportation offers "no eye
for the unusual" (AN ix). The greatest disadvantage though, the author-
narrator claims, is that it does not allow for unplanned adventures,
travelling on public transportation dictates when and where one goes. He
states:

> To travel by schedule is not to travel at all, but to be transported, like a
> piece of baggage . . . To be able to go only where the train or bus chances
> to take me, at the time the train or bus chooses to go—no, that is not to
> travel. Go by train or bus and you may become a much-travelled man. You
> will not, cannot be a traveller. (AN x)

This type of argumentation is in line with much travel literature from the
early years of car travel; people complained about rigid timetables and
fixed, inflexible routes (Houston 2009, 31; Coulbert and Youngs 2013,
111). The same argumentation goes for travel by sea and air, it is
expedient but has little to do with travelling (AN x). Mere transportation

by bus, train, ship or plane fails to meet the requirements of "travel for its own sake" (AN x).

The author-narrator indicates that this travelogue is not about simple transportation from a point of departure to a planned destination, as would be the case for a sedentary traveller. The author-narrator and his wife have no plans but want to go wherever they fancy. However, one big concession is made in relation to the ultimate means of travel. They do not travel on foot, but by car. The car provides its owners with a freedom that cannot be matched by trains or buses. Car travel provides flexibility as Mike Featherstone explains:

> The term automobility works off the combination of autonomy, and mobility. . . . The autonomy was not just through the motor, but the capacity for independent motorized self-steering movement freed from the confines of a rail track. The promise here is for self-steering autonomy and capacity to search out the open road or off-road, encapsulated in vehicles which afford . . . speed and mobility. (Featherstone 2005, 1—2)

By car the author-narrator gains access to long-distance travelling while enjoying freedom from schedules and strict itineraries. The car is loaded with the necessities needed for independent travel, and everything superfluous is discarded in a nomadic vein. A new journey is started with a large tent and everything needed to set up camp. Thanks to the car the author-narrator and his wife are free to travel as the whim takes them.

The introduction concludes by distinguishing between "travel as a means to an end, and travel as an end in itself" (AN x). This travelogue, it is clear, builds on the classic difference between a traveller and a tourist, with the author-narrator positioning himself firmly in the former camp. In his understanding of the concept of a traveller, the author-narrator focuses on travelling without itineraries and plans, and the ultimate goal to see the world from the others' perspectives. This goal may be interpreted as being in line with Islam's concept of the nomadic traveller. *Auto Nomad in Sweden* is about "hopeful travel—travel for its own sake; it is also the story of a car, and of her nomadic owners" (AN x). The hope that he suggests brings associations of the open road and all the possibilities that it promises, not least becoming truly and intimately acquainted with Sweden and its people.

Their car is a Standard Twelve, a 1938 model. However, this is not a mere impersonal motorized carriage, this is the Black Beetle. She is more than a car; she is a faithful friend with a name of her own. The Black Beetle is introduced to the reader in no uncertain terms. Comparing her to other cars on the ferry from the UK to Sweden it is said that "the Black

Beetle, had she not been so modest, could have silenced them all" (AN 2). In this brief statement the author-narrator hints at the car's long history as a co-traveller and transforms the inanimate construction into a living entity by personifying her.

The account then describes the Black Beetle's battle-scars from long-distance travelling through France, Switzerland, Italy and Sicily. Further she has traversed the African continent from the northern coast all the way to Cape Town under difficult conditions. This very experienced car is no stranger to danger, "On two occasions she had only just avoided rubbing shoulders with a rhino and she had wandered far over veld tracks and by game paths through the bushveld in Zululand and the Transvaal and the Orange Free state" (AN 2).

The author-narrator's rendering of the Black Beetle's hazardous pre-war experiences from the roads in many countries on two continents not only establishes her credibility, but by implication, also his. The car's adventurous, independent streak mirrors and reinforces the very same quality in its master. Mimi Sheller argues that a "car materializes personality and takes part in the ego-formation of the owner or driver as competent, powerful, able and sexually desirable" (Sheller 2005, 225). Whereas this travelogue is virtually void of sexual references, the first three adjectives describe the author-narrator's persona well. It is he who has steered her through storms and on dangerous roads over deserts and wilderness. The record of the author-narrator and the Black Beetle's prior journeys, avoiding even the faintest trace of planned and scheduled transportation, confirms the author-narrator's already established position as a traveller and a nomad in the sense of travelling without plans and schedules, roaming widely.

The personification of the Black Beetle continues throughout and serves to demonstrate the close bond between the car and her master. This bond is further underpinned by the numerous snap-shots of the Black Beetle in the book. The author-narrator's focus on documenting the car's presence, rather more than on his young wife's, gives evidence of how important the car is to him. The car is bestowed with human feelings and performs human activities. As a true friend she looks out for her master, she lies "unobtrusively guarding the back of the tent" (AN 78), she continues to serve him well as she works on "doggedly, banging and bouncing and slewing" (AN 130) on terrible roads, and she is "in spite of her years . . . ready for adventures" (AN 255). She is a veteran and knows everything about bad roads, "The Black Beetle suddenly found herself on a familiar surface—badly corrugated earth" (AN 25); her experience even stretches to wild-life photography, "a technique that the Black Beetle knew well of old. I switched off the engine, declutched and let her coast gently along, while Joan . . . felt for the cameras" (AN 100).

The personification of the car helps to construct the author-narrator's identity as a traveller in the sense of his roaming and wandering around. This nomadic aspect is further accentuated as the author-narrator claims that he is no longer the master of the Black Beetle; she is the one that leads while they follow, "We had come to Sweden to wander wherever the car might take us" (AN 152). This statement follows immediately after a long passage about the nomadic life of the Sami people in the far North, where the nomads follow their reindeer. This structure implies that the auto nomads follow their cars like the Sami people follow their herds.

The importance that the author-narrator attaches to the roaming aspect of his understanding of being a nomad is also expressed in his portrayal of the open road and the numerous opportunities it offers. Approaching Sweden the Black Beetle's owners are eager to see new lands. "Hitting the road" symbolizes freedom at long last for the author-narrator; it is the first time since the Second World War that the Black Beetle heads out for adventures abroad:

> now she was really free. Now she was headed for the open road again; footloose and free.

> "No plans," we had said. "We go wherever we fancy". . . . We were interested in one thing—the open road. No more—no less. (AN 2)

Not only does the road offer them freedom of mobility, it also enables them to leave a country suffering from a number of restrictions in the aftermath of the war. By labelling the road as "open", the author-narrator hints at the vast number of possibilities offered. The open road is a place where all kinds of scenery and landscape can be experienced, where one can meet all kinds of people, where all kinds of unforeseen things happen; the open road is a place of adventure. Further, it offers the freedom to follow a nomadic life style. In addition, the open road holds a promise of discovering the other and the self.

Setting out, the author-narrator claims that their minds are "comfortably blank" (AN 3), they are free to absorb whatever they will meet on the road, something that is a necessity in reaching the aim to get to know a country and its inhabitants. To have an open mind and curiosity are necessary prerequisites to being able to take a Swedish perspective, to cross lines, to become-other in Islam's sense.

The author-narrator aims to get to know the other along the open road, but not all roads are equally good for this in his opinion. He claims that the authentic Sweden is only to be found in the countryside. This is a romanticized notion of where to find Swedish authenticity.

The two travellers hit the road, both literally and metaphorically; they constantly try to get away from the most convenient roads, stating that "direct roads had no special charms for us" (AN 27). In leaving the beaten track they seek to meet with "ordinary" Swedes and to cross lines, and therefore qualify as nomadic travellers. As sedentary travellers, they would instead have chosen the most convenient roads as they would be easier to handle and would bring them from one point to another much faster. As nomadic travellers, the author-narrator and his wife instead take side roads; they take detours and also leave the road for paths so narrow that the Black Beetle can barely cope:

> The track divided. We took the left fork, turned left again at a little clearing where several tracks converged, halted at another fork and found only footpaths ahead. One was too narrow even for the Black Beetle, so we took the other and pushed hopefully on, twisting and wriggling between the tall, straight trunks. (AN 29)

Leaving the beaten track to travel without plans poses trials of various kinds. They take the wrong road and become lost, they cannot continue and are forced to turn, sometimes they do not quite know what to do, and just "hope for the best" (AN 32). They do not always know where they will find a place to stay the night, "It was cold, we were tired and hungry, and there was no sign of the *vandrarhem*" (AN 102).

From the road they observe a multitude of things from a distance— landscapes, various buildings, their first reindeer; they see people going about their everyday business in the fields or in more industrial settings; they see men walking bulls, and a woman gathering blueberries. Far from tourist attractions they see the way in which ordinary people live.

Not all encounters are at a distance though. During the breaks from driving, making coffee or preparing meals outdoors, people join them for a brew or a smoke. The author-narrator and his wife interact with the locals whenever possible. When the break is over they take to the road again, filled with impressions while free from personal attachments and consequences; they will in all probability never meet these people again. However, these interactions with people who go about their every-day lives make them experience the country and its inhabitants at a very personal level. Consequently, the detours they take are not detours in a literal sense; on the contrary, they are, the author-narrator suggests, the routes to local cultures, to the authentic Sweden. However, the question remains, do the routes lead

to an intimate knowledge and understanding of the Swedes and all things
Swedish, to a proper crossing of borders in a nomadic vein?

Negotiating Borders between Self and Other

Arriving in Sweden the auto nomads have crossed a national border. They
come from a country deeply affected by war where the inhabitants still
suffer from restrictions of various kinds, not least the rationing of food.
They compare their country of destination with the one they have left
behind. Their first glimpse of Sweden holds a promise of structure and
orderliness, but above all, of abundance. From the ferry they observe their
fellow passengers going ashore:

> we climbed to the top deck to watch a swarm of emancipated humanity
> pour ashore into their promised land. Judging by their behavior on board
> ship, the promise that excited them most was of gastronomic delight
> without limit and the rediscovery of forgotten flavours. To such
> elementaries can humanity be brought in a few short years. (AN 4)

A little later, the author-narrator and his wife also succumb to the
temptations of the table. Entering a shop in Gothenburg, Joan is rendered
speechless by the overwhelming impact of the abundance of all sorts of
food, listed in painstaking detail:

> Joan was speechless. The shelves were heaped high with an unimaginable
> profusion of food—food in packets, food in tins, food in bottles and jars.
> The floor space was lined with crates of oranges, grapefruit, bananas,
> tomatoes, apples, pears, peaches, eggs. There were enormous hams, and
> rows of tongues, and pressed meats, and sausage meats. It was a
> gastronomic fairyland. (AN 8)

Having completed their shopping they go to the flat of their new-found
friends from the Swedish Institute to "eat and eat and eat" (AN 9). The
memory of the meal, the author-narrator states, lingers on "because of . . . its
complete freedom . . . Everything was set upon the table and we went,
butterfly-like, from flavour to flavour with no orderly sequence" (AN 11).
Not only does this comment serve to underline the contrast between scarcity
and abundance, it also echoes the already established differentiation between
scheduled transportation and travelling the open road.

   Such is the initial meeting with Sweden, a country that stands in sharp
contrast to Britain. This contrast is clearly marked through a discourse of
difference. They observe and they compare—however, whatever insights

they gain remain on a superficial level, comparing as they do only the most immediate observations.

Now, this is only a first impression of Sweden. During their subsequent journey they make efforts, with varying success, to stay true to their belief that travel should lead to getting to know a country and its inhabitants intimately.

From the driver's seat of the Black Beetle it is possible to observe both the towns and the landscapes that they pass through. These observations give rise to reflections on country and inhabitants in a discourse of difference, in this case in the form of positive comments on the Swedish political system, in contrast to that of Britain. The author-narrator writes in a well-established tradition in his rendering of the north. Interwar accounts had already promoted the Nordic countries as "happy countries" (Stadius 2013, 244). They "offered an example of how peaceful, comparatively wealthy and democratic societies could become reality" (Ibid., 242). Sweden's implementation of a third-way politics meant a compromise between capitalism and communism; it was a "kind of rational compromise between the best of two worlds, built on pragmatism, piecemeal reformism and a feeling for the common good in the welfare of the people" (Andersson 2009, 232). Sweden was at the time busy building its *folkhem* (People's Home) and, according to Jenny Andersson, it

> functioned as a kind of utopia in European politics . . . the utopia of the rational, pragmatic society where social problems are approached in a non-dogmatic and efficient way, and where the great conflicts of capitalism—combining efficiency and equality, markets and society—somehow found their utopian solution. (Andersson 2009, 232—233).

This image of utopia is confirmed by the author-narrator. The Black Beetle passes through Eskilstuna, which the author-narrator explicitly compares to Sheffield. Observing "Sweden's Sheffield" (AN 41), he reflects on the issue of equality:

> We saw no signs of industry, no sallow-faced men in dirty dungarees at this hour—twelve-thirty—when in any industrial town you might expect to see men going home at the end of their shift or coming out for their lunch-break. But the Swedish steelworker is like any other Swede; he is not a special class in a long and complex ladder of classes. His day's work done, he becomes an ordinary citizen, well washed, dressed in clean clothes, and ready to enjoy his leisure in any way he fancies. (AN 42)

Such reflections contribute to a discourse of difference as they implicitly compare a culture of equality to the author-narrator's own British background with a "complex ladder of classes". The Swedish worker is described as "an ordinary citizen", implying that this is not the case for his British counterpart. Further, it seems that "in any [British] industrial town" one would expect that industrial workers would bear the marks of unhealthy work environments and dirt, something that is not the case in Sweden. This othering of the Swedish worker is unequivocally positive, and in this way the author-narrator contributes to building the image of Sweden as a haven of democracy. *Auto Nomad in Sweden* is certainly not the first travelogue or report to promote such an image. Peter Stadius, discussing the interwar period in Europe, claims that the perception of the Nordic countries as "happily excluded from economic crisis, social unrest and political tension [was] widely repeated in testimonial narrations from this region" (Stadius 2013, 241), something that Andersson argues continued also after the war, as the positive image of Sweden was

> strengthened by the affirmations and confirmations that throughout the post-war period [came] from foreign observers, who [saw] in Sweden something deeply desirable that unfortunately for various reasons was not within the realm of the possible in their own political context. (Andersson 2009, 232)

Later when the Black Beetle and her owners reach Sandviken, another clean and wholesome-looking town, the author-narrator continues his socio-political comparison with Britain and thereby the process of othering. He states that

> the enormous advantage of the dispersal of Swedish industry is nowhere better seen; there are no concentrations into hideous black areas, spelling damnation not only to the countryside but to the unfortunate people condemned to be born and to live and die there. (AN 59)

He contrasts the much preferred dispersal of industry in Sweden with concentrated, hideous black areas, bringing to mind the industrial landscapes of the Black Country in the Midlands.

Not only towns trigger such contemplation, also the open landscapes, through which they pass, set off reflections. Idyllic villages nestle close to minor industries and the author-narrator muses on how such a societal structure brings enormous benefits to the Swedes, claiming that there is an "enormous increment of human happiness that accrues from this scattering of industry throughout the country" (AN 73). He further comments that "the smaller unit has prevented the violent cleavage between urban and rural areas and interests and has given the urban dweller easy access to all the amenities of the countryside" (AN 73). Such observations are found in the official presentation of Sweden published by the Swedish Institute, in which it is claimed that the "industry is out in the country [and that] a striking aspect of Swedish industry is that there is so little of it in cities" (Svenska Institutet 1947, n.p.). The reported impressions of the towns and landscapes serve to reinforce the author-narrator's belief in the blessings of the Swedish model, and, by contrast, his lack of belief in the system he comes from. Further on he concludes that in

> Sweden there is a delicate balance between private enterprise and State ownership and that balance is created not by theorizing but by practical common sense. In the final analysis what is practical, what is expedient, what is economically sound is the course adopted. (AN 116—117)

This notion of practicality is something that the author-narrator remarks upon throughout the trip, claiming that "if a thing is practical in Sweden it requires no other justification" (AN 53). Into this practicality the political third-way fits perfectly, he argues, discussing contemporary Swedish housing schemes, "Men are encouraged to build their own homes and develop their smallholdings with government loans and assistance, individual ownership of land and property being accepted in the Social Democrat system" (AN 86). This self-reliance is, by far, preferable to spoon-feeding, and he notes that "Sweden, fortunately, has been wise in this respect" (AN 86). The author-narrator portrays Sweden as different from Britain by othering the country and its inhabitants, evaluating them in a very positive light. Through a discourse of difference he confirms the contemporary view of Sweden that many Europeans had, at the same time as he criticizes much of Britain's socio-political structure.

However, this othering often leads him to fail in crossing the lines. One example is when he comments on how Sweden's left hand traffic with left handed driven cars (until 1963) results in ludicrous and even dangerous situations:

> There is one comic result. Being unable to make hand signals, they rely upon the trafficator alone and so thoroughly is its use dinned into them that I declare no Swede could make a turn without using it. . . .

> There are more serious results.

> Seated away from oncoming traffic, the Swedish driver is a menace when he has to overtake; he is even more of a menace when he makes a right turn; for up comes his trafficator and still he hugs the left of the road instead of coming on to the crown and letting overtaking traffic pass on the inside. (AN 64)

He continues to describe Swedish driving, furnishing details about the process of overtaking. All his information has an ethnocentric point of departure—he generalizes from his limited observation, referring to "they", "the Swedish driver" and "he", and thus resorts to the use of stereotypes. However, one thing is to view the other from an ethnocentric perspective, quite another is to judge the other's behaviour as deviant. The author-narrator points out the "normal" way of doing things by othering the Swedish driver's behaviour, "instead of coming to the crown", which would be the correct (British) way. Doubtless, an additional aspect of the description of Swedish driving habits is the need to entertain the readers. Poking mild fun at behaviour that deviates from a norm may indeed create some amusing scenes.

Also in other parts, written to convey information and knowledge about the Swedish people, the author-narrator reveals difference through the means of stereotyping. Here he adopts an essentialist approach to Swedish culture, for example, when he claims that "cleanliness and Sweden are synonymous" (AN 84), or when he goes so far as to divide the Swedes into "quite distinct types" (AN 114).

Occasionally, the author-narrator tries to look behind the stereotypes to give an explanation of why the Swedes—in his opinion—have a special essence. In the following example his othering is marked by less favourable comments. After having presented education in Sweden, which he claims starts quite late, he states:

> In general . . . the Swede is naturally slow to develop; his reactions are far from swift, he is not merely deliberate but often maddeningly, painfully slow . . . there is no doubt that Swedish reactions are slow, and the explanation may lie in a century and a quarter of unbroken peace. In all that time the country has lived free from war and enjoying the steady increase of prosperity that comes from continued peace. Freedom from fear and freedom from want, however desirable in themselves, may have undesirable results. (AN 114—115)

From his ethnocentric perspective the author-narrator has learned that Swedes are sedate. He ascribes them the specific property of being "slow", and evaluates this as highly negative, "maddeningly, painfully slow". Later he claims that the Swedes' slow reactions are a matter of concern. They can lead to dangerous situations on the road, "It is worth noting, if only as a warning to other motorists of what to expect in Sweden!" (AN 115).

Such a concrete reference to Sweden's dangerous traffic serves to confirm his diagnosis of the Swedes' sedate nature. He continues by trying to understand the underlying reason for this state of affairs. He takes historical facts into consideration and concludes that "unbroken peace" is detrimental to the development of a quick mind. His effort to try to understand the reasons for the Swedish behaviour that he has witnessed may be seen as a first step towards crossing the line. However, his argumentation is developed in a discourse of difference, and draws on his continuing stereotyping of the Swedes.

As we have seen, in the reflections about Sweden triggered by what he witnesses from the car, the author-narrator takes an essentialist approach to Sweden and the Swedes, focusing on the differences between Sweden and other countries. In this he behaves as a sedentary traveller. His reflections may be helpful for the reader, but they do not really contribute to a change of perspectives.

In some instances though, the author-narrator modifies this essentialist approach:

> He [man in tourist bureau] knew no English; but the Swedes we met seemed to have a genius for understanding. If we did not follow them immediately they tried again—in different words, very quietly. (AN 32)

The use of "seem" and the restriction "the Swedes we met" qualify the validity of his statement. In his rendering of this personal encounter, and referring to other similar meetings, the author-narrator moves beyond a purely stereotypical description. He comments only on those individual Swedes he has met and not on an entire population. In this he comes closer to crossing lines than he does with the essentialist approach.

Avoiding stereotyping is one way of attempting to cross the lines, another way is to overcome the language barrier, and for the author-narrator and his wife to learn to speak Swedish. Moving with an open mind along the road also means gradually moving into a language. With curiosity, openness and a willingness to learn Swedish, the process goes quite smoothly. Their language proficiency is, in fact, confirmed in an interview published in a local Swedish newspaper, asserting that the MacArthurs had mastered the intricacies of the Swedish language to an astonishing degree in such a limited period of time (Pier 1946, 1). It starts with Joan repeating what she hears a customer asking for in a shop, "she just listened to what the woman said, memorized the words and repeated them when her turn came. It worked" (AN 26). From this initial stage their language skills develop rapidly and with the help of a small dictionary they are soon able "to keep the conversation going" (AN 48). This enables them to get to learn to know the other "intimately" and "sympathetically". In one particular conversation with their hostess Fru Vallberg, for example, they learn about her perspective on the terrors of war and on the role that Sweden played during that time:

> Here, from a working-woman in a humble home in the country, was deepest sympathy and a keen desire to be of service; we began to realize something of the feelings of the ordinary Swede, forced to look on at the titanic struggle and to realize his helplessness in face of the terror that stalked through Europe. (AN 48)

In this personal comment on Fru Vallberg's account, the author-narrator expresses the sympathy and understanding that he and his wife develop, as they "began to realize something of the feelings of the ordinary Swede". Through the conversation with their hostess they have crossed a line. The author-narrator suggests that they have learned something new, moved forward and established a sense of community. However, while moving forward he moves backwards, as he falls into the trap of stereotyping. For him Fru Vallberg becomes the representative of "the ordinary Swede". So whether their conversation in this case actually leads to any intimate knowledge remains a moot point.

Whether successful or not in becoming-other, the author-narrator and his wife understand the role language plays in intercultural encounters. It is the key to understanding the others' perspectives and to changing one's own perspective; and the fact that language skills serve as a door opener to the other culture becomes increasingly obvious along the road. During their trip they immerse themselves in the Swedish language to the extent that they eventually discard feelings of "strangeness" and "strain":

> It was only when we were going to bed and so relapsed into English that we realized that from the moment we got up we had been in the company of Swedes who knew not a word of English, that we had talked with them almost without pause and had felt neither strangeness nor strain in their company. (AN 177)

Here they meet and communicate with local people without, they claim, experiencing them as "other" in relation to themselves. In this situation the earlier so prominent discourse of difference has been substituted for a discourse of similarity.

The importance of language in crossing lines is further stressed by the narrative about their meeting with a British woman who refuses flat out to speak Swedish:

> Almost the first thing we heard was:

"My dear, I can't speak a word of Swedish. I don't even try!"

So we retired discretely to some armchairs and had a chat with a young Swedish couple until the way was clear. There are times when one's fellow-countrymen—and, as in this case, countrywoman—are not entirely welcome. (AN 210)

Rejecting such an attitude, the author-narrator and his wife try to avoid any contact with her. The British woman displays a complete lack of openness towards her unfamiliar surroundings and thereby also disrespect for the other culture. She behaves as a sedentary traveller, remaining firmly rooted on her side of the border, unwilling to respond to otherness.

The value of mastering Swedish is underlined in many episodes. The further they move from the southern urban areas, the more excitement they are met with over them being British, often only revealed by the GB registration of the Black Beetle. British travellers had been scarce in Sweden during the war for obvious reasons. With their fast developing mastery of Swedish, they are taken for Danes, because of their accent, and in one case even for Norwegians. The last situation leads to a complete confusion of borders.

In the far north they meet a young man from the south of Sweden. At the hostel they talk together for an entire evening, in Swedish, something that gives rise to a misunderstanding about their respective nationalities. The author-narrator and his wife presume that the young man is Norwegian due to his accent; he, on his side, assumes that they are Norwegian, due to their accent. The mistake is not cleared up until the next morning. The author-narrator realizes that they "had talked at cross purposes all evening" (AN 104), something that turns out to give them insights into the self-image of the Swedes in relation to the country's policy of neutrality during the war. The author-narrator claims to have learned that the Swedes felt accused by the Norwegians for having indirectly supported Nazi-Germany and "neutrality had grown shameful" (AN 104) in spite of all the support the Swedes had given to other people during and after the war. In the conversation the Swede adjusts to the others, the supposedly Norwegian author-narrator and his wife. He takes their accusatory attitude for granted, and praises the Norwegian war effort, while he slights Swedish politics, but not without trying to elicit some sympathy for Sweden's position. Since the author-narrator does not display the hostile attitude that the young Swede might have expected, it may be that he feels free to elaborate more openly on the complex post-war position of Sweden and its inhabitants' identity. Language proficiency, in this case, leads to mistakes that give insight, something that in turn may result in the crossing of borders.

However, not all social intercourse is dependent on a common language to cross lines. Another way is by simply sharing in the local people's activities. Such sharing creates a special intimacy. The author-narrator and his wife have to leave the road every evening to find somewhere to sleep—arrangements vary from their erecting their large tent on camping sites, to hostels and even to private homes into which they are generously invited. When the reader is told about the meeting between the couple and their host(s), the focus is generally not on language but rather on the sharing of daily chores, overcoming any cultural barriers and potential feelings of awkward otherness. This is especially true for the females along the route, "Joan and Fru Vallberg and little Gun-Britt went to work in perfect harmony to prepare supper" (AN 47). South-African Joan, together with the Swedish hostess and her daughter, both of whom she has only just met, set to work side by side. This results in an effortless bridging of any cultural borders and creates an intimate closeness between the three that does not need a common language. Such encounters entailing the sharing of work and chores build friendship, and the author-narrator and his wife who are bound to take to the road again, do this with some regret:

> "We'll come back," I reassured her, and she smiled again. But she was very sorry to say even *au revoir* to her little *hus-assistent*, as she called Joan. . . .
>
> [S]he was not merely the *förestånderinna* of the *vandrarhem* and the lady who ran the little hotel; she was already a friend. We were sorry to leave her. (AN 118)

They do return after a sojourn to the far north, but then, inevitably, have to leave again:

> She wrung our hands. It had been a great pleasure to have us. She would not forget her little *hus-assistent*, although she did not suppose she would ever see us again. One of the odd and, in some way, saddening aspects of a nomadic existence is the unexpected attachments that can so swiftly be formed. (AN 154)

This chance meeting with the Swedish hostess has a great impact on the author-narrator and his wife, and they feel enriched by it. This is what they set out to do—to get to know a country's inhabitants intimately and sympathetically. They have come to know their hostess and she has become a friend. Through their meeting, they have to some extent changed, become-other. This change has, however, an emotional cost for those constantly on the road.

Early on the author-narrator states that he and his wife "who had promised, so casually, to come to Sweden were already very different people" (AN 55) because of their meetings with individual Swedes. He claims that they have changed even more before they return to Britain. At the very end of the travelogue, there is a sentimental comment that serves to confirm the author-narrator's perception of himself as a nomadic traveller and of what he has learned about life in Sweden:

> It [the burning down of a farmhouse] is a tragedy that must be fairly common in Sweden; nevertheless it was affecting, and there was something particularly poignant about this destruction of a little lonely farmhouse now that we had come to know so well the life that centred round such homes as these. (AN 263)

His being on the road—off the beaten track—and his open mind have led the author-narrator away from tourist attractions towards encounters of various kinds with Swedes in their daily activities. In this sense he has come close to the people and reached his goal.

Concluding Remarks

With the help of Islam's categorization of the sedentary vs. the nomadic traveller, we set out to answer two interrelated research questions vis-à-vis *Auto Nomad in Sweden*. First, what does the open road signify to the author-narrator? Second, to what extent does the open road lead to a change of the author-narrator's self?

As we have shown in our analysis, the open road for the author-narrator is the place where he can reach his goal of getting so close to the Swedes that he gets to know their perspectives and thereby changes himself. This is also a goal that he shares with the nomadic traveller in Islam's sense. In Islam's theory, nomadic travellers aim to overcome the boundaries between themselves and the other. The author-narrator is convinced that travelling along the open road will lead him to the countryside and here, he assumes, he will find the authentic Sweden. Here he voices a romanticized notion about where the real culture of a country can be found.

The countryside is idealized as an idyllic place with attractive features such as lake shores, gardens and parks (AN 73). It is an area of morality, in contrast to the urban area with its pubs, cinemas and street corners (AN

73) that have a demoralizing impact on people (AN 59). The countryside, the author-narrator suggests, is the natural environment in which people may develop their full human potential. This environment stands in stark contrast to the urban areas in which people are emotionally stunted. His argumentation is basically flawed, ignoring as he does, that the city is an inherent part of any modern culture. In addition, without the city and its technological developments, his Standard Twelve would never have seen the light of day.

Let us now turn to the next question concerning how the author-narrator responds to differences he meets along the road. In the travelogue we have identified two types of discourse. On the one hand, there are descriptive passages where the author-narrator conveys knowledge about Sweden and the Swedes. In his description of the socio-political system in Sweden, for example, the author-narrator promotes a positive counter-image to Britain. For the people back home in Britain it may be difficult to imagine that such a system could function. Other passages contain practical advice for those readers who plan to set out on similar trips through Sweden. In these passages *Auto Nomad in Sweden* is perfectly in line with traditional travel guides. In these parts where the author-narrator conveys knowledge of various kinds, he focuses on differences between Sweden and Britain, showing an essentialist approach to culture. In these passages the author-narrator behaves as a sedentary traveller.

However, it must be remembered that the author-narrator was commissioned to produce a travelogue, and also supported by the Swedish Institute. In addition, he wants to prepare a readership that wants to set out on a similar trip. This context may explain why he makes full use of a discourse of difference, in spite of the fact that such a discourse clashes with his personal goal.

On the other hand, there are passages where the author-narrator tells his readers about his personal encounters with people. These narratives document his attempts to cross lines and see the world from the Swedes' perspectives. The author-narrator and his wife take every opportunity to talk with people they meet along the road. Two approaches can be identified in these attempts to cross lines. One is the immersion in the Swedish language. The author-narrator realizes the role language plays: Language can be the door to another culture. Learning a country's language can open up for other ways of thinking, other ways of seeing the world. The second approach is the sharing of daily chores with their hosts. This creates an intimate closeness between especially the females along the road, a closeness that builds friendship. In these narratives of their personal encounters there are glimpses of them as nomadic travellers in the sense of Islam. Through MacArthur's travelogue we see how the author-narrator moves between being a sedentary traveller and trying to be a nomadic traveller. While the former is related to his commission to write a book to entice Brits to travel to Sweden and provide them with useful tips, the latter is connected to his personal endeavor to change and gain the Swedish perspective. His transformation may not be profound, but he has at least made an effort to cross the lines, and may to some extent have changed. In the end, however, one may wonder whether it is at all possible for an auto nomad, constantly on the road, to get to know the other "intimately" and "sympathetically".

References

Andersson, Jenny. 2009. "Nordic Nostalgia and Nordic Light: the Swedish Model as Utopia 1930—2007". *Scandinavian Journal of History*, Vol: 34, No. 3, 229—45.

Ayrshire History. 2000. Ayrshire History, accessed January 14, 2016, http://www.ayrshirehistory.org.uk/postings1/macarthur.htm

Coulbert, Esme, and Tim Youngs. 2013. "Introduction". *Studies in Travel Writing. Special Issue: Travel Writing and the Automobile*, Vol: 17, Issue 2, 111—15.

Featherstone, Mike. 2005. "Automobilities: An Introduction". In *Automobilities*, edited by Mike Featherstone, Nigel Thrift, and John Urry, 1—24. London: SAGE.

Houston, Kerr. 2009. "'A proper medium': Early motorists' perception of the European landscape". *Early Popular Visual Culture*, Vol: 7, No. 1, 29—43.

Islam, Syed M. 1996. *The Ethics of Travel. From Marco Polo to Kafka*. Manchester: Manchester University Press.

—. 2014. "Traveling the Times of Empire". In *Travel and Ethics. Theory and Practice*, edited by Corinne Fowler, Charles Forsdick, and Ludmilla Kostova, 204—15. New York: Routledge.

MacArthur, Wilson. 1948. *Auto Nomad in Sweden*. London: Cassell & Co. Ltd.

—. 1950. *Auto Nomad in Barbary*. London: Cassell & Co. Ltd.

—. 1951. *Auto Nomad through Africa*. London: Cassell & Co. Ltd.

—. 1953. *Auto Nomad in Spain*. London: Cassell & Co. Ltd.

Pier. 1946. "Skellefteå, a pleasent [sic] place förklarar vittberest skotte". *Skellefteåbladet* (Skellefteå), Aug.13, 1 and 3.

Sheller, Mimi. 2005. "Automotive Emotions: Feeling the Car". In *Automobilities*, edited by Mike Featherstone, Nigel Thrift, and John Urry, 221—42, London: SAGE.

Stadius, Peter. 2013. "Happy Countries: Appraisals of Interwar Nordic Societies". In *Nordic Experience: Communicating the North: Media Structures and Images in the Making of the Nordic Region* (3rd ed), edited by Jonas Harvard and Peter Stadius, 241—62. Farnam, Surrey: GBR Ashgate Publishing.

Svenska Institutet. 1947. *Introducing Sweden.* Stockholm: Svenska Institutet.

CHAPTER THREE

"TRAVELLING NORTH TOGETHER" THE NORTH, WHALES, AND INTERCULTURAL COMMUNICATION IN KATHLEEN JAMIE'S ESSAYS AND POEMS

MELANIE DUCKWORTH

Introduction

"Going North" is a central preoccupation in the work of Scottish poet and essayist Kathleen Jamie. "Travel" and "the north" are recurring themes in her work, from her earliest published poems to her latest collection *The Bonniest Companie* (2015), and her lauded essay collections, *Findings* (2005) and *Sightlines: A Conversation with the Natural World* (2012). "The north", for Jamie, is a resonant concept, signifying sometimes Scotland itself, and sometimes a broader, transnational identity, evinced in the phrase from the poem "Arbour": "May is again pegged out / across the whole northern hemisphere . . ." (*BC* 22).[1] Jamie represents the north as a shared home not just for humans, but for whales, birds, stones, plants and oceans. Her essays and poems are filled with journeys, overwhelmingly in a northward direction. The journeys are both literal and metaphorical, mundane and mythical. She describes her own journeys, but also refers to the historical journeys of whalers, Romans, and Celtic saints, and the ordinary yet astonishing journeys of whales and birds. Ultimately, the north is not just a home but a dream and ideal, as Jamie comments: "there is always farther north" (*S* 15).

---

[1] For ease of reference, I use abbreviated book titles to distinguish Kathleen Jamie's published collections: *The Tree House* (2004): TH; *Findings* (2005): *F*; *Waterlight: Selected Poems* (2007): *W*; *Sightlines* (2012) S; *The Bonniest Companie* (2015): *BC*.

In this paper, I look at the progression and development of northward journeys in Jamie's work, a progression in which her gaze moves steadily beyond the human. "Going north" begins as a site of intercultural communication, but in her later work, journeys to the north provide opportunities to question the boundaries between culture and nature. It is tempting to view culture and nature as opposed to one another and mutually exclusive. As Jonathan Bate points out, however, the earliest meaning of the word "culture" was not so removed from the natural world:

> The earliest meaning of "culture", which endured from the middle English period to the end of the eighteenth century, was "a cultivated field or piece of land". In late middle English, the primary sense shifted from cultivated land itself to the action of cultivation: the word referred to tillage, the working over of the soil. (Bate 2000, 3)

Thus culture was not so much the opposite to the natural world as rather an ordered response to it.

For Jamie, both "travel" and "the north" are sites of communication between cultures, but they also function as metaphors *for* cultures, in particular the transience and mutability of cultures. The long view Jamie takes in her work, looking back to Neolithic settlements and forward to a time when our own civilization is in ruins, engenders a sense that culture is fragile and finite. In addition to this, as her work progresses, the boundaries between "culture" and "nature" become increasingly unclear. One goal of "travelling north" is to journey beyond the reach of culture, to nature's most remote and pristine states. But Jamie's essays reveal that this dream is impossible. Culture and nature are intertwined; they cannot be prized apart. As Jamie points out in a review of *Four Fields* by Tim Dee:

> There has been much talk recently of "nature writing". It's a problematic term because "nature" itself is impossible to define, and also because our best "nature writers" are equally concerned with culture, and the fact that we live immured in both. We exist and communicate within nature and culture—neither offers escape from the other. (Jamie 2013)

Going north raises questions about who we are, where we belong, and where we are going to end up. In Jamie's later work, the "we" referred to in these questions expands significantly to encompass not only human cultures, but also animals and the natural environment.

Intercultural communication, while not the sole focus of her work, impinges on it in a number of ways. The journeys she describes offer moments of contact with different cultures—not only those of the locals but of other travellers. In the essays of *Findings* and *Sightlines*, Jamie also encounters cultures which are lost, such as the stone age monument at Maes Howe, and the abandoned village and medieval chapel on the island of Rona. She thus partakes in a kind of one-sided "intercultural communication", reading the signs that have been left, standing in the same landscapes and rooms, experiencing similar weather and effects of the light to those long ago. She does this with one eye on the past and one on the distant future, asking "what, if the world lasts, would people five thousand years hence find worth saving of our age?" (Jamie 2005, 21—22). More hauntingly still, the journeys Jamie takes are overlaid by the ghosts of previous journeys: saint Rona arriving on Rona hundreds of years ago, villagers abandoning remote Scottish islands for the last time in the early twentieth century, whaling ships navigating north in the nineteenth century, geese flying to their nesting grounds every year. These multiple journeys resonate with her own, mapping cultural identities that are provisional, transient, and fluid.

This paper comprises four sections. The first, "Scotland", discusses the ways in which Jamie invokes travel and the north when depicting and interrogating the cultures of her homeland. This is the part of her work where "intercultural communication" can most clearly be seen, as Jamie demarcates cultural rifts between Scotland and England, and within Scotland itself, particularly between generations and between genders. The second part, "The Remote and Archetypal North", discusses the ways in which Jamie invokes the "romance" of "going north", only to gently, and wryly, deconstruct it. In the two final sections of the paper I turn to the remarkable ways in which Jamie engages with whales. In "Whalebones" I borrow some terminology from the field of material ecocriticism to discuss the detailed and nuanced ways Jamie discusses these relics. Jamie uncovers instances when whalebones have functioned as strange emblems of intercultural communication, but the stories they embody go far beyond this, to the lives and the deaths of the whales themselves, and to the ancient and abiding ocean in which they live. In the final section, "Whales", I concentrate on moments in which Jamie's own journeys to the north intersect with the journeys of whales. The northward journeys of people and animals become emblematic of a shared home and a shared fate.

Scotland

The field of intercultural communication considers not only the logistics and difficulties encountered when people from different languages and cultures communicate with each other, but also the ways in which discourses actively construct versions of the self and the other. As Ingrid Piller puts it:

> Culture is an ideological construct called into play by social actors to produce and reproduce social categories and boundaries, and it must be the critical research aim of a critical approach to intercultural communication to understand the reasons, forms and consequences of calling cultural difference into play. (Piller 2011, 16)

Some of these "reasons, forms and consequences" are explored in Jamie's iconic early poem, "The Queen of Sheba", which playfully questions Scottish cultural identities and cultural production. In this poem she uses cultural difference to highlight the limitations of a certain Presbyterian Scottish perspective which advises young women not to think above their station: ". . . Stick in / with the homework and you'll be / cliver like yer faither / but no too cliver / no above yersel" (*W* 87). It plays upon the phrase "who do you think you are, the Queen of Sheba?", the purpose of which is to question the status and validity of the person to whom it is addressed. In response, Jamie imagines the Queen of Sheba herself arriving on a fabulous northern journey into Scotland: "Whit, tae this dump? Yes!" (Ibid., 85). She is opulent and astonishing and in all ways beyond the small-town cultures through which she travels:

> *All that she desires, whatever she asks*
> She will make the bottled dreams
> of your wee lasses
> look like sweeties. (Ibid., 86)

Despite this, the Queen of Sheba is fascinated with Scotland: "she wants to strip the willow / she desires the keys // to the National library" (Ibid., 87). The freedom, confidence and opulence of the Queen of Sheba inspire the Scottish girls who encounter her, and when she receives the inevitable question, "whae do you think y'ur?":

> . . . a thousand laughing girls and she
> draw our hot breath
> and shout:
> THE QUEEN OF SHEBA! (Ibid., 88)

Thus Scotland in this poem is the destination of a journey from the exotic south, and "intercultural communication" enables young Scottish women, the "thousand laughing girls", to reassess their own culture and imagine more liberating ways of existing within it.

In "Gloaming", Jamie comments on a cultural identity projected onto Scotland and other northern nations: "This is the North, where people, the world perhaps likes to imagine, / hold a fish in one hand, in the other a candle. / I could settle for that" (*TH* 20). In her poetry, however, Scotland emerges as a place home to multiple cultures, divided by language, class, gender and generation. In "The Graduates", Jamie describes her generation as "emigrants of no farewell", who "remember no ship / slipping from the dock" but "have surely gone", retaining their old language only in jokes and fragments (*W* 41). Education has transported them to another land:

> And my bright, monoglot bairns
> will discover, misplaced
>
> among the bookshelves,
> proof, rolled in a red tube:
> my degrees, a furled sail, my visa. (Ibid., 42)

Here, the Scots word for children, "bairns", lightly emphasizes that due to the speaker's own invisible journey through education, her children's culture and languages do not mirror her own.

The metaphor of the journey becomes a way of articulating Scotland's multiple cultural identities. Journeys also emerge as instrumental in the ways in which Scotland's northerness is ascribed and experienced. In *The Bonniest Companie*, which is based on poems she wrote each week in 2014, the year of the Scottish referendum, Jamie explores the ways in which Scotland's northerness has been mythologized. In "Glacial", she imagines the Romans arriving in Scotland but thinking better of it: "too much grim north, too much faraway snow" (*BC* 4). "Scotland's Splendour" describes the experience of discovering in a charity shop an edition of a book of photographs she had as a child, crammed with "page after page of mountains / mirrored in placid lochs, / cattle ambling by reedy lochs, stags on heather-moor" (Ibid., 49). The book had been a gift to her family for their "sojourn among the southern", as her parents had moved to England for a number of years. Jamie had not yet learned to read, but poured over the pictures of the "hardback nation":

> —a dream-tinged land we pick up,
> then shelve again, a place
> so difficult and faraway
> I grat miserable tears the day
> my folks announced we were flitting,

turning north again,
back to thon unknown cold stone 'home'. (Ibid., 50)

The poem describes a reluctant journey north back to Scotland. For the child Jamie, Scotland was a land that "declared itself" in their speech, but apart from that just existed in pictures. The final lines of the poem slip partially into Scots: "grat . . . flitting . . . thon", enacting a curious amalgamation of outsider and insider perspectives on Scotland, as the speaker remembers her childhood tears at the thought of a northern land "so difficult and far away".

Even for inhabitants of the south of Scotland, the "north" can be somewhat of a dream. In the poem "Bonaly", again about her childhood, Jamie recounts a memory from her school sports day:

> . . . All for the greater
> glory of Bonaly, our House, denoted
> by a red sash and named for a loch
> somewhere high in the Pentlands—
> a place we could scarcely imagine. *Bonaly!* (*W* 59)

Here the name of a loch far to the north is shouted enthusiastically by children who have never been there. Thus, in a variety of ways, Jamie aligns Scotland's identity as northern with descriptions of and allusions to journeys: actual, potential, remembered, metaphoric, historic and mythological. It is through journeys that Scotland is experienced as northern, but journeys also gesture towards the hybridity and multiplicity of Scottish identities. In Jamie's work, however, journeys to the north often also indicate a desire to travel into remote and elemental nature, although Jamie goes on to complicate, question, and redefine this ideal.

The Remote and Archetypal North

In the poem "Lochan", first published in *Jizzen* (1999), "going north" is imagined as a kind of freedom or escape into wilderness, almost an escape into another world. Jamie writes: "When all this is over I mean / to travel north, by the high // drove roads and cart tracks, / probably in June . . ." (*W* 70). The poet means to find:

> A certain quiet lochan
> where water lilies rise
>
> Like small fat moons,
> And tied among the reeds,

Underneath a rowan,
A white boat waits. (Ibid.)

In this poem, the imagined journey to the north is one-directional. The end of the journey as related here is a quiet lake, where a "white boat waits", presumably to take one further still. The speaker imagines travelling quietly away from civilization, deep into nature and myth. As David Wheatley points out, the "white boat" has a "Gaelic echo": "the *bád bán* being traditionally the emigrant ship" (Wheatley 2015, 53). A similar tone can be found in "The Whale Watcher" from *The Tree House*, in which the speaker, also dreaming of a journey that may take place in the future, declares: "And when the last road / gives out, I'll walk" (*TH* 25). The poem describes a wish to camp out in "some battered / caravan" all summer long, watching the ocean:

till my eyes evaporate
and I'm willing again
to deal myself in:
having watched them

breach, breathe, and dive
far out in the glare,
like stitches sewn in a rent
almost beyond repair. (Ibid.)

While "Lochan" is mythical in scope, "The Whale Watcher" expresses the quiet hope that the existence of the whales indicates that the world is not quite lost. Matt McGuire argues that the poem relates to Jamie's ideal of a "walking-pace world", and that "her recent volumes bring us closer to the natural world, to re-establish a sense of intimacy with the outdoors, to rediscover an interdependence that has been forgotten amidst the onrush of our contemporary age" (McGuire 2009, 148, 147). It is tempting to read these poems as a turning towards nature, and a turning away from culture, but in her work as a whole, this is something Jamie refuses to do.

The two poems discussed above describe imagined journeys: idealized, archetypal journeys. The journeys north described in the essay collections *Findings* and *Sightlines* are quite different to this. For a start, they are all return journeys. Jamie travels to various locations in the north: remote northern Scottish islands, Greenland, and Norway; but she always comes home again. A second difference is that all these journeys are to named places. They exist firmly in the real world and the present moment. In these remote places she encounters scientists, ecologists, restoration workers. If "Lochan" describes a metaphorical journey to the north, these other journeys are quite literal.

While critical of idealistic representations of "northern-ness" Jamie admits to feeling some of the romance of the north herself. In the opening essay of *Sightlines*, she notes: "When the party's assembled we begin trudging inland over crisp plants quite new to me. I've long loved the word 'tundra', with its suggestion of far-off northern emptiness, and I guess these must be tundra plants, under my feet" (*S* 2). Despite admitting a love for the remote and elemental idea of the north, when she gets there, "emptiness" is not what she finds. In her journeys to the north, she encounters locals, scientists, other tourists, the remains of ancient civilizations, dolphins, whales and birds. She encounters stone, ice, wind, plants, but also bones, broken string, lighthouses, oil refineries, and even, in the remotest places, winking satellites. She is not alone.

The opening and closing essays of both *Findings* and *Sightlines* focus specifically on journeys to the north. In "Darkness and Light", the opening essay of *Findings*, Jamie writes: "I imagined travelling into the dark. Northward—so it got darker as I went. I'd a notion to sail by night, to enter into the dark for the love of its textures and wild intimacy" (*F* 3). The essay is set around the time of the winter solstice, and Jamie is attempting to reclaim a positive perspective on darkness in contrast to its associations with sin and death. A journey north seems just the way to do this, and she quotes the Orkney poet George Mackay Brown, that "Nowhere . . . is the drama of dark and light played out more starkly than in the north" (Ibid., 23). Jamie travels up to the Orkney islands, seeking "pure, natural darkness", and finds herself repeatedly frustrated by the insistent lights of human presence, impossible to escape. In the end she reconciles herself to this:

> There was much sound: wind, and waves, but also a silent light show: the beams of many lighthouses shone and faded shyly across the water, each to its own pulse. The pathways they made on the black surface of the sea slipped in and out of existence. Here were all the textures of darkness— bulwarks of land, shifting sea, dark starry sky, and the consolation of lighthouses. And in the distance, among further dark islands, rose the flare-stack of the Flotta oil refinery. Oil is brought there from the North Sea fields by tanker or pipeline, and by day and night excess gas is burned off into the atmosphere, in an orange flame. (Ibid., 26)

Seeking natural darkness, the poet is confounded by human lights, but in the seascape described above, another kind of beauty is discovered: the entanglement of darkness and light, remoteness and civilization, industry and dreams.

Whalebones

The figure of the whale is another way in which Jamie interrogates the slippery boundaries between culture and nature. In the final two parts of this paper, I would like to concentrate on the figure of the whale as emblem of, object of, and finally participant in, journeys to the north. Whales are a haunting presence in *Sightlines*, explored particularly in the essays "The Hvalsalen" and "Voyager, Chief". These essays focus on the bones of whales found on beaches, displayed in museums, and erected around Scotland and northern England as whalebone arches. One such arch can be found over Jawbone walk, a footpath in Edinburgh. Jamie notes that it was brought down from the Shetland Islands as a prop for an exhibit as part of the 1886 International Exhibition of Science, Art and Industry. The whalebones formed a tent as a backdrop for an exhibition of Fair Isle knitting: young women from the north were shipped down "six at a time" to demonstrate their wares (*S* 222):

> To citified visitors, the whole ensemble must have spoken of "northern-ness", of whales and fish crofts and spinning. An idealized vision, of course . . . The girls are lovely, but it's the ghost presence of the whales which is arresting, both in the photograph and today, for real, in the Meadows, with no drapery, and with buses and pedestrians passing by. As for the animals, well, they were sent up in the chimneys of the nineteenth century. Science, Art and Industry, all of it smoothed and lit by whale oil. (Ibid.)

The 1886 exhibition becomes a site of intercultural communication between "remote" northern Scotland and "citified visitors". The whalebones are present as an exotic backdrop; they are emblematic of an "idealized vision" of northern Scotland that includes wild landscape, handcrafts and whales. For Jamie, however, the "ghost presence of the whales" signifies more than this (Ibid.). She points out the nineteenth-century reliance on whale oil, which was fatal for the whales themselves. Her essay goes on to worry at the function of whalebones as cultural markers, and to explore different ways of apprehending them.

The whalebone arches erected around the coasts of Scotland and Northern England function as strange cultural markers on the landscape, bearing histories of, among other things, intercultural communication. Jamie discovers that curiously, the whalebone arch at Whitby is a gift from Alaska. It is the jaws of a bowhead whale, once known as a "right whale", as Jamie puts it, "the right whale to hunt" (Ibid., 226). Its numbers were seriously depleted by European whale hunters in the 19th century and it is now protected, but "Alaskan Eskimos are licensed to hunt a quote of bowheads a year" (Ibid.).

> A board beside Whitby's arch explains that the jawbone was a gift from the people of Alaska. It was flown over from Anchorage and received with all due Yorkshire pomp and ceremony, and unveiled by Miss Alaska herself. It was given to replace an older arch, which had likewise been a gift—that one from the king of Norway, but which had weathered away. This is strange, this gifting of whalebones between nations. Whale jaws and pandas. (Ibid.)

Here, then, is another way in which whalebones function as a strange form of intercultural communication. The gifting of whalebones between nations appears to be a recognition of a shared historical, geographical and cultural identity, one built on a history of whaling. But the bones speak not only of the cultures of whaling nations and histories of slaughter, but of the bodies and the presences of the whales themselves:

> The more you find of these relics, the more you look at them, indoors or out, the more they seem imbued with a particular presence. Whatever it is, a whale arch is not a triumphal arch; these are not trophies. All these bones, regardless of the species, share a solemnity and slightly luminous quality. (Ibid., 228)

The whalebones do not merely signify "northern culture" but remain relics of the lives of the whales themselves. In her consideration of the multiple histories and stories embodied in the bones of the whales, Jamie performs what can be described as a form of "material ecocriticism".

Serenella Iovino and Serpil Oppermann describe "material ecocriticism" as the ecological branch of "the intellectual movement known as the 'new materialisms'" (Iovino and Oppermann 2012, 75). The "new materialisms" began as a reaction against the "period of dismissal of materiality as the main result of the so-called 'linguistic turn,' namely, the view that language constructs reality" (Ibid., 75—76). Paying new attention to matter itself, new materialist critics work on the premise that "the true dimension of matter is not that of a static and passive substance or being, but of a generative becoming" (Ibid., 77). Quoting Karen Barad's *Meeting the Universe Halfway* (2007), they explain:

> In other words, matter "is not a blank slate," or "immutable or passive," but "*a doing, a congealing of agency*;" and Barad calls it "*a stabilizing and destabilizing process of iterative intra-activity*" (*Meeting* 151). She further proclaims that "[m]atter is neither fixed and given nor the mere end result of different processes. Matter is produced and productive, generated and

generative. Matter is agentive, not a fixed essence or property of things" (*Meeting* 137). (Ibid., 77)

To see matter as "agentive" is to see it as capable of "agency": of acting and affecting the world. Whalebones, as Jamie discusses them, are a particularly apposite example of "agentive matter", as they both affect the world around them in the way they are collected, erected and gazed-upon, and are affected by the world, as they weather, age, and change over time.

Iovino and Oppermann identify two ways of carrying out "material ecocriticism": firstly, focusing on "the way matter's (or nature's) nonhuman agentic capabilities are described and represented in narrative texts", and secondly focusing on "matter's 'narrative' power of creating configurations of meanings and substances, which enter with human lives into a field of co-emerging interactions" (Ibid., 79). While it would be possible to identify many examples of the former in Jamie's poems, in her essays about whalebones she performs the latter. In her descriptions of whalebone arches in Edinburgh, Whitby, and the Scottish Isles, Jamie teases out stories embodied in and overlaid upon the bones. As Iovino and Oppermann put it:

> Matter, in all its forms, in this regard, becomes a site of narrativity, a storied matter, embodying its own narratives in the minds of human agents and in the very structure of its own self-constructive forces. Interpreted in this material-ecocritical light, matter itself becomes a text. (Ibid., 83)

In her essays about whalebones, Jamie reads whalebones as texts, and muses upon the way others read whalebones as texts. In "The Hvalsalen" she describes her northward journey to Bergen, where she discovers a nineteenth-century collection of whale skeletons in the Bergen Natural History Museum. The collection is another testament to international and intercultural communication—the specimens had been collected by and exchanged between several nations. A restoration team from Yorkshire, Sweden and Denmark work on restoring the skeletons. Gordon, a Yorkshireman, is intrigued by the nineteenth-century metalwork by which the whales hang from the ceiling: "And these chains! Look at them! It's part of the thing—it's like the whales were giants that had to be restrained. They're all handmade . . . You couldn't do it now. The way I see it, this Hvalsalen is a monument to the whales—their only monument—but it's testament to those working men too" (*S* 109—110). Jamie can see his point, but to her "the bolts and nails still looked Frankensteinian" (Ibid., 110). The stories narrated by the "text" of the bones tell of both movement and entrapment, freedom and slaughter. The whalebone arches standing on coastlines, and skeletons collected in museums, are not the sole preserve of either culture or nature. They embody the blurring and layering of the two.

When encountering the skeleton of a whale, it is impossible not to try to imagine the body of the whale, and to think about how it moved. Standing within the jaws of a blue whale skeleton, and glancing back over its massive length, Jamie conducts a "thought experiment": "Despite the size, you could, with a minimum of effort, extend your sense of self, and imagine this was your body, moving through the ocean. You could begin to imagine what it might feel like, to be a blue whale" (Ibid., 115). As well as imagining herself into the bodies of the whales, Jamie begins to imagine what they can *hear*. Some of the strangest and loveliest whale relics she encounters are the whale eardrums collected in museums. Jamie describes one collected in a kind of "cabinet of wonders" in a tiny museum in Stromness:

> And next to the hair balls is something shaped like an open purse, the size of your cupped hands. It's thick but hollow, and wrapped over on itself, with one lip tucked under the other, leaving a fissure. It is a vessel made of the densest bone, and is smoothed and rounded as though it had rolled in the ocean for a long time. Because of the gap, it is somewhat like a mouth. However, it wasn't made for speaking, but for listening. The label reads, "Whale's ear drum". (Ibid., 232)

Jamie says: "I find them beautiful and sad and complete; all that can be said about sea-waves and sound waves, song and utterance is rolled together in these forms" (Ibid., 233). The eardrums are particularly poignant because of their function for the whale: they are small, round objects that once used to hear. Jamie points out that the jaw bones of the whales also were a part of this process, picking up vibrations from the ocean and transmitting them to the whales' internal ears. This produces the compelling image of all the arches erected on the coast, and eardrums nestled in museums, as not merely producing meanings, but *listening*. Jamie asks: "What did they hear, these jaws, these eardrums? They heard us coming, that's what" (Ibid., 233). Whale bones are more than tokens to be exchanged between nations, or to be erected as monuments to northern cultural identities. Jamie is not content to speak *with* whalebones, nor even to merely decipher them. She wants to speak *to* them, *through* them, to the whales themselves.

Whales

Towards the end of "Voyager, Chief", Jamie asks: "What else did the whales hear, with their huge eardrums? They heard a sea change. The beginnings of deliverance. They'd have heard, felt, the drill bits biting into the seabeds, oil tankers sliding over the surface above, signaling a development in human technology" (Ibid., 234). The new human reliance on oil, which, of course, has its own environmental implications, means that whale oil is no longer needed and that whales are no longer hunted to the extent they were in the past. She writes: "I suggest that if they cared to listen, if we could indeed whisper into those eardrums, they'd hear something, at least in this country, like atonement" (Ibid., 235). As well as describing encounters with whalebones in her journeys to the north, Jamie documents a few memorable encounters with the whales themselves.

In the final section of this paper, I concentrate on Jamie's observation that not only people travel north—animals do too. Material ecocriticism recognizes the agency of the non-human, and one way to explore this is to reflect upon the journeys of non-human animals. Jamie's poetry emphasizes the fact that animals are also travellers. She has many poems about migrating birds: some which migrate up to Scotland from homes far south, and some, like the Arctic geese, who winter in Scotland and then fly back to the Arctic in the summer. She also reflects on the journeys of whales, as well as the journeys of those who hunted the whales. By imagining herself into the bodies of animals, Jamie envisions a different kind of journeying altogether. In "Voyager, chief", she remarks: "I suppose I'd always half known that there is a whale presence in these islands. Or, put the whale's way, these islands are a surprising, sometimes disastrous presence in the sea" (Ibid., 220). Imagining the British Isles as potentially disastrous to whale journeys changes one's perceptions of centre and periphery.

Intercultural communication focusses on communication between humans, but it may not be completely erroneous to discuss intercultural communication between animal species, too. Greg Garrard notes that "[w]ithout minimizing the evident differences from human cultures, ethologists are content to use the term 'culture' to describe non-genetically transmitted behavior such as the varied hunting practices of orca or regional differences in primate tool-making and interaction" (Garrard 2012, 157). When Jamie sights her first group of killer whales, she assumes the male is in charge, but learns otherwise:

> I read later that orca live in family groups, and that what I'd assumed, with
> slight world-weariness, was a dominant male with one or two adult females

and his offspring, was nothing of the kind. They are matriarchal; a son
remains with his mother. In a year or so, god willing, my son will indeed
be taller than I am. When he measures himself against me, and gloats, I'll
poke him in the chest and say, "Just be glad you're not a killer whale, pal".
(*S* 86)

Killer whales have their own "culture", which can be misinterpreted in
much the same ways human cultures can, as we interpret the world with
ready-made assumptions about how it works.

Some of the most moving moments in *Findings* and *Sightlines* are
moments at which humans and animals are—however briefly—travelling
together. The following year, on a different island, Jamie encounters the
killer whales again. Spotting a group of killer whales of the coast off
Rona, Jamie experiences a thrill of recognition—the S shaped curve of the
largest whale's fin seems to be exactly the same as a whale she saw years
earlier, on Noss. It seems impossible, but a biologist confirms that it is
probably true—photographic evidence shows that the group of whales she
sees from Rona matches those recorded several times around Shetland at
the time she was there.

"Believe what you see", say the eye-trained naturalists. Aye, right. Most of
the time you'll sound like an idiot. But once in a blue moon you might be
right. You just might be making the same journeys as these other creatures,
all alive at the same time on the same planet. (Ibid., 208)

Jamie encounters the killer whales with two of her friends, and they
scream and shout and race about the island in their excitement, until at
last: "all we could do was jump and shout as the four animals travelled on
through the surf zone northward, with the cliff at their right sides, and their
vast Atlantic domain to their left" (Ibid., 200). The whales are also
travelling north. This detail is recorded with a naturalist's precision, but
the frequency with which Jamie's writing mentions "north" adds to a
multifaceted picture of the north as a shared home and a shared
destination.

The incident described above is a good example of what I refer to in
my title: "Travelling North *Together*". Jamie's poems sometimes revisit
episodes described in her essays, an example of which I shall consider
shortly. When comparing Jamie's treatment of the same episode in prose
and poetry, it is instructive that she does not poetically "edit out" other
people from her encounters with nature. A very different approach can be
seen in the famous example of William Wordsworth's "I wandered lonely
as a cloud". Wordsworth describes going for a walk, completely alone,
and encountering a field full of daffodils. He is amazed, and has a

spiritually uplifting experience that he carries with him throughout the rest of his life: "it flashes on my inward eye, that is the joy of solitude" (Wordsworth 2006, 305). When one reads about the same incident in Dorothy Wordsworth's journal, however, which uses many of the same words and images, and was written several years earlier, one discovers that William was walking with his sister and a friend when he encounters the daffodils (Dorothy Wordsworth 2006, 396). When discussing this poem with my students, I always ask, why doesn't he mention this? The answer, of course, is that Wordsworth is writing about a very particular kind of "Romantic" experience, the premise of which is being *alone* in "nature". Jamie refuses to do this. The encounters Jamie describes in her essays and poems remain shared experiences. This is very deliberate. In a review of Robert MacFarlane's *The Wild Places*, which she entitles "A Lone Enraptured Male", Jamie questions the absence of people from his adventures (Jamie 2008). She suggests that in his search for "wildness" he misrepresents a peopled landscape, and silences voices other than his own:

> Such lovely honeyed prose. Macfarlane is delightful literary company, polite, earnest, erudite and wide-ranging in his interests. It's rather wonderful—like an enchantment on the land. In place after place, the length and breadth of the country, there is "wildness". There are no meetings, no encounters with intrusive folk. It is all truly empty, secret and luscious. From Sutherland to the Burren, even to Dorset and Essex, the book reveals a sense of beguiling solitude. There are no other voices, no Welsh or Irish or differently accented English. It has to be thus, of course, because if we start blethering to the locals the conceit of empty "wild" will be lost. So there has to be silence, an avoidance of voices other than the author's, just wind in the trees, or waves, the cry of the curlew. (Ibid.)

In contrast to MacFarlane and Wordsworth, Jamie does not write other people out of her encounters. As discussed in the first section of this paper, in her descriptions of journeys to the north, she engages with the cultures of locals, tourists, scientists, and long-lost civilizations. Her reflections on whalebones unpick some of the delicate and brutal ways in which culture, nature, and meaning are enmeshed. She continues this careful listening to both culture and nature in her depictions of animals and people travelling together.

The final essay of *Findings*, "Cetacean Disco", describes an encounter with about forty "white-sided dolphins", as well as some whales, on a tourist boat leaving from the Ilse of Mull. The boat is manned by three Scottish boys in their twenties, who, Jamie remarks, "[a] century ago . . . would have been the very men putting out with the whalers, out of Stromness and Stornoway, to get themselves locked up in the Arctic ice.

Now, for a fee, they were showing the whales to us" (*F* 186). The dolphins they encounter are not normally seen in those parts, and it is an experience of much jubilation. The dolphins come and swim alongside the boat, and watch the people watching them, and for a time, they all travel north together. Jamie revisits this experience in the poem "White-sided Dolphins", where she writes: "just for a short time / we travelled as one // loose formation . . ." (*W* 17). The "we" here includes the tourists on the boat, flat on the deck with their cameras, and the dolphins themselves. Here it is not just humans observing dolphins, but the inverse too. The dolphins

> took it in turn
> to swoon up through our pressure-wave,
> careen and appraise us
> with a speculative eye
>
> till they'd seen enough,
> when true to their own
> inner oceanic maps, the animals
> veered off from us, north by northwest. (Ibid.)

Like the killer whales, the dolphins disappear towards the north. This very literal description of travelling together is echoed in the essay "La Cueva", in *Sightlines*, when Jamie travels, south this time, to see Paleolithic carvings of animals deep in a cave. The cave had been rediscovered around 100 years ago, when farmers noticed bats entering and leaving the cave:

> Different needs for different eras. Our Paleolithic kinship with animals, with nature, is over, broken, or so we say. Strange, though, that it should have been animals—bats—who led the way to the cave this time round. And that it should have happened just as we were discovering a new relationship, closer than ever: discovering that we'd all travelled together, separating and overlapping, out of a deep, shared evolutionary origin.
> The lamps shift again. The shadows lope. Incredibly, we are going on, farther still. (*S* 171)

Here Jamie questions the modern assumptions of human exceptionalism and alienation from the natural world. Humans and animals have a shared identity and a shared origin—like Jamie and the dolphins, we are on a shared journey.

Sightlines ends with a stranger and bleaker vision, which Jamie reworks into a poem in *The Bonniest Companie*. In "Migratory I" a whooper swan lies dead, its head resting slack on the turf "pointing north like a way sign" (*BC* 39). What does this mean? As with the whales whose bodies provided the bones which form the arches erected along the Scottish and northern English coastlines, the swan's very literal journey has ended, and its body has become a metaphor. But of what? It is, as Iovino and Oppermann would put it, "storied matter" (Iovino and Oppermann 2012, 83). Jamie's interpretation of the swan's body as a "way sign" makes it strangely agentive (*BC* 39). Where is it pointing? Home? Emptiness? Death? An uncertain future? Or, simply, further north? Its wing is so marvelous that Jamie reflects that it is like "a radiant gate / one could open and slip through" (Ibid.). This is impossible, however, and the poem leaves the reader with the image of being totally overwhelmed by wind, "half elated, half scared" (Ibid.). The essay goes on, and closes with the image of Jamie and her companions being air-lifted away from the island in a helicopter, which reminds Jamie of the swan's final northward journey. If we are on a shared journey, where does it end? Travelling north together becomes a reminder of the vulnerability of the world we know and depend on: "a wing's beat, and it's gone" (*S* 242).

References

Bate, Jonathan. 2000. *The Song of the Earth*. London: Picador.

Garrard, Greg. 2012. *Ecocriticism: The New Critical Idiom*. 2nd Edition. London and New York: Routledge.

Iovino, Serenella and Serpil Oppermann. 2012. "Material Ecocriticism: Materiality, Agency and Models of Narrativity." *Ecozon@: European Journal of Literature, Culture and Environment*, Vol: 3, No. 1, 75—91.

Jamie, Kathleen. 2015. *The Bonniest Companie*. London: Picador.

—. 2013. *"Four Fields* by Tim Dee—Review." *The Guardian*, Saturday August 24, accessed January 24, 2017, https://www.theguardian.com/books/2013/aug/24/four-fields-tim-dee-review

—. 2012. *Sightlines*. London: Sort Of Books.

—. 2008. "A Lone Enraptured Male." *London Review of Books*, Vol: 30, No. 5. March 6, accessed January 24, 2017, http://www.lrb.co.uk/v30/n05/kathleen-jamie/a-lone-enraptured-male

—. 2007. *Waterlight: Selected Poems*. Saint Paul, Minnesota: Grey Wolf Press.

—. 2005. *Findings*. London: Sort of Books.

—. 2004. *The Tree House*. London: Picador.

McGuire, Matt. 2009. "Kathleen Jamie." *The Edinburgh Companion to Contemporary Scottish Poetry*, edited by Matt McGuire and Colin Nicholson, 141—53. Edinburgh: Edinburgh University Press.

Piller, Ingrid. 2011. *Intercultural Communication: A Critical Introduction.* Edinburgh: Edinburgh University Press.

Wheatley, David. 2015. "'Proceeding Without at Map': Kathleen Jamie and the Lie of the Land." *Kathleen Jamie: Essays and Poems on her Work*, edited by Rachel Falconer, 52—61. Edinburgh: Edinburgh University Press.

Wordsworth, Dorothy. 2006. "From *The Grassmere Journals*." *The Norton Anthology of English Literature*, 8th Edition, Vol: 2, edited by Stephen Greenblatt et al., 392—402. New York and London: Norton & Company.

Wordsworth, William. 2006. "I Wandered Lonely as a Cloud." *The Norton Anthology of English Literature*, 8th Edition, Vol: 2, edited by Stephen Greenblatt et al., 305. New York and London: Norton & Company.

CHAPTER FOUR

TRANSLATION BETWEEN CULTURES IN THE FIELD OF TRAVEL

MARIA SELEZNEVA

Communication between people from different cultural backgrounds entails communicating from different cultural perspectives. The fact that cultures differ means not only that people differ, so do their environments. Environment here refers not only to climate and weather conditions, but also to historical events, religious beliefs and cultural values. Tourists who go to a foreign country for their vacation usually notice differences between their own culture and the one of the host country. However, not all tourists are able to discern similarities and familiar concepts when they compare their own culture with the other. We all have our own perspective of the world. This perspective is created in the process of various complex events in our lives. Even though we live in one world, every single one of us perceives the world from a unique vantage point. This paper claims that translators who present a foreign culture compare it to their own culture. This method is called "domestication" in the field of translation and paradoxically it helps to pinpoint the differences of a foreign culture compared to one's own. In this paper we shall explore how translators present Russian cultural aspects, such as ice, snow, cold and long winters, in texts for foreign tourists.

Texts for tourists are indeed expressions of attempts at intercultural communication. Translators may here constitute bridges between two, or more, cultures and their main goal is to make a foreign culture understandable and attractive for tourists. This is particularly true in situations where translators' decisions can influence the recognition of a whole foreign culture. Translators have to solve numerous problems to achieve their main goal, among others they need to avoid creating stereotypes and negative associations with a foreign culture. The main challenge for translators, hindering the understanding of a foreign culture, is culture-specific concepts. Let us take a closer look at this challenge.

Problems of Translation in the Field of Tourism

Culture-specific concepts are also called realia. Realia represent elements
of local and historical colour (Vlahov and Florin 1980, vi). These concepts
are frequently the cause of translation errors, or at least translation
problems. Thus, they require special attention from the translator. Three
issues in particular need to be addressed: First, why do these realia create
difficulties for understanding? Second, how may they be transferred from
one culture to another in a comprehensible way? Third, what exactly is it
that is transferred?

Firstly, a particular cultural concept might exist in a foreign culture,
but there is no name for it. Baker explains that this is the case when a word
is known in a foreign culture, but not "lexicalized" in its language (Baker
2011, 18). Consider, for instance, the Russian word "kapel". The word
"kapel" is a special phenomenon associated with early spring in some
regions in Russia when water drips from icicles because of warm and
sunny weather. The word "kapel" can also mean a special sound produced
by water drops dripping from icicles on a warm day after a long Russian
winter. The phenomenon this word expresses might exist in some English-
speaking countries, but it will by necessity not have the same connotations
for English speakers as for Russian speakers. In this case translators have
to use descriptions of the term "kapel". The translators are here mediators
between the foreign, Russian, culture and the foreign readers of their texts.
It follows therefore, that translators should carefully interpret texts taking
into account both the author's intention and cultural-specific features. That
is why, apart from being experts in the linguistic aspects of a culture,
translators should also have thorough knowledge about other aspects that
create a culture, for instance historical or geographical facts. Authors of
texts may create a special atmosphere or they may symbolize some
essential features of a particular cultural place in their writings. An
example would be that the word "spring", in the minds of those who live
in Russia, is associated with new life, nature again awakens after a long
and cold winter. Thus, "kapel" is not just a geographical/meteorological
phenomenon, but also a cultural concept, which creates a special
atmosphere related to the season of spring. If the translator knows just the
linguistic meaning of the term, then all the cultural connotations of the
word might be lost.

Secondly, sometimes a concept may be completely unknown for
foreign readers of a translated text about a specific culture. Such concepts
are also culture-specific. For instance, on a website about Russian culture
a particular religious tradition is described in the following way:

While most bundle up to brave against January's frigid temperatures, Russians of the Eastern Orthodox faith put on bathing suits and plunge through holes carved in frozen lakes and rivers (or a "Prorub") as part of the yearly Epiphany Celebration. (Bivens, n.p.)

The Russian term "prorub" as seen from the context of the example above refers to the tradition of the Catholic Orthodox Church. In many countries people drill holes in the ice of frozen rivers and lakes to fish, but it is only in the regions of the Russian Federation that people drill these holes for religious celebrations, plunging themselves into the ice-cold water. This tradition reminds believers in the Catholic Orthodox Church of the christening of Jesus Christ. The lack of an equivalent word made the translator in this example use an explanation of the term for foreign readers. Indeed, such a tradition as the one described in the above text might be both unknown and also quite exotic for readers who live in warmer climates. Therefore, additional information about the religious importance of the tradition will serve to prevent misunderstandings of this particular foreign custom on behalf of English speaking readers. The general meaning of the culture-specific word "prorub" ("holes drilled in frozen rivers") is clearly rendered in the text.

Thirdly, the source language and translated language can make "different distinctions in meaning" (Baker 2011, 19). Thus, in some regions of the Russian Federation people distinguish between different types of snow and ice. For example, "pozemka" (some particles of snow created not by snowfall, but blown by the wind along the ground covered with snow), "protalina" (a place where snow is melting and one can see the soil), "porosha" (snow which was falling at night and stopped in the morning), "pad" (big snowflakes which do not allow one to see the light) "nast" (the crust of ice over snow), "izmoroz" (another type of hoarfrost which appears on thin and long items during foggy and frosty winter weather). Such variation is irrelevant, for example, to many British people—at least for those who live in the southern parts of Britain. At the same time, the British stereotypically have a broad range of names for various types of rain. All these groups of words create problems for translators who aim to help readers to a thorough understanding of a foreign culture through their texts.

Fourthly, sometimes the translated language does not have a specific term for a foreign concept (Baker 2011, 20). For instance, the Russian word "pechka" is usually translated into English as "stove" or "oven". However, these words can be perceived differently in different cultures. The traditional Russian "pechka" is a major cultural phenomenon and is even used as a character in Russian folklore fairytales. Bivens, writing on a Russiapedia website about Russian culture, says:

> The heart of the traditional rural Russian home used to be a large, brick stove that took up about nearly one-quarter of the living space of a peasant home. The immense structures weighed between one and two tons and served multiple purposes. (Bivens n.p.)

Although Bivens translates the word "pechka" as "stove" or "oven", the Russian "pechka" is hugely different from a common "stove", something which is clear from the context in the above description of the term. Apart from being used for cooking, "pechka" was also a warm place for sleeping, especially in cold winter nights in the past. The "pechka" can still be found in houses in remote Russian villages.

The Translator's Decisions in the Field of Tourism

In translation, just as in a dialogue, translators and their readers should speak one language. However, a translator's mother tongue limits his or her ability to present foreign elements in an unaffected way. Translators, as opposed to tourists, are not constantly on the move, they return to the domestic cultures for which they translate. Translators presenting a foreign culture for a target culture inevitably domesticate the former. Domestication in translation is a strategy of "ethnocentric reduction of the foreign text to receiving cultural values, bringing the author back home" (Venuti 2008, 15). In other words, a domestication strategy in translation entails an adaptation of a foreign culture to the culture of the readers and the translator's mother tongue. While some scholars see a problem in domesticating foreign concepts, we believe that domestication can be a helpful strategy in translation in the field of travel and tourism. Domestication is meant to create a balance between familiarity and strangeness, between the culture of the Other and the culture of the Self. A domestication strategy in translation is meant to achieve an understanding of a foreign culture by readers of the translated text. Tambiah, Rosman and Rubel argue that any culturally bound word can be translated into another language based on a "bridgehead of understanding" or a common ground between cultures that makes intercultural communication possible (Tambiah et al. in Sturge 2007, 20). In fact, foreign and domestic cultures always have common features whatever the level of cultural distance that exists between them. To find a common ground between cultures means to make intercultural communication possible. That is why it may be argued that there are three levels of common ground between a foreign and a domestic culture. This common ground can be also called a "kinship" between cultures (Rosman and Rubel in Sturge 2007, 22).

According to this classification, kinship between two culturally bound notions can be complete, partial or zero in translation. When the kinship between terms is complete it means that there is a solid "bridgehead" in the form of a common notion. In other words, the language of the translated text does not have a hyponym, but has a hyperonym. Thus, a translated notion can be general, but fully transparent for the readers of a translated text. Examples of the first level of kinship can be various items of clothing, which in different cultures have different specific features, and thus they differ in names. For instance, the Russian word "ushanka" becomes more understandable if the translator renders it with its hyperonym—"hat". However, foreign readers would not know that this hat is worn in winter and that it is an "ear-flap" hat.

The second level of kinship refers to notions that can be translated with an approximate comparison between a foreign and a domestic culture. This comparison is very often subjective because it is usually based on the translator's own view of kinship between foreign and domestic notions. These notions often do not have an exact hyperonym. The next example illustrates this type of kinship:

> In Russia and across the Slavic world, the season of the winter's end has been celebrated since Pagan times and since the onset of Christianity, the great festival of Maslenitsa, like Carnival, has marked the coming of the Great Lent. (Fernandez, n.p.)

Only replacing the one term, "Maslenitsa", with another term, "Carnival", will not be sufficient, because the two words are not exact equivalents. However, using a simile, "like Carnival", in this sentence makes the image of a traditional Russian celebration more clear and understandable.

Kinship of the third level concerns "the internal logic" (Rosman and Rubel in Sturge 2007, 22) of a term. In other words, within the field of tourism the translator has to become a researcher and delve deep into the tastes, sounds or any other structural aspects of a concept which is to be translated. Subjectivity is difficult to avoid in this case, but it is possible if the translator focuses on the description of the observable features of the concept. Examples, already mentioned, would be "pozemka" (some particles of snow created not by snowfall, but blown by the wind along the ground covered with snow) and "protalina" (a place where snow is melting and one can see the soil).

Hallett and Kaplan-Weinger claim that discourse is created through "the similarity between things that are said and written in different texts about the same aspect of reality" (Hallett and Kaplan-Weinger 2010, 5). These similarities assist in reconstructing the knowledge that they express (Hallett and Kaplan-Weinger 2010, 5). At the same time, there is the belief that any idea usually has a basis in a form of a universal truth. The belief can be supported by Grice's maxim of quality, where one tries to be truthful, and does not give information that is false or not supported by evidence (Penn Arts and Sciences 2016, n.p.). The basis of any idea can refer to general notions of traditions, beliefs, and historical facts. However, all cultures, apart from having similarities in the form of universally accepted truths, also have their own specific differences.

According to Gadamer, differences can be accepted if representatives of a culture are ready "to look beyond what is close at hand" (Barthold, n.d.). Thus, "understanding requires an act of will by which we transpose ourselves into the horizon of the other" (Barthold, n.d.). The theory of horizon shows the way in which representatives of different cultures should communicate between each other. No cultures are untouched by other cultures, this is especially true for our globalized world. Understanding between people from various cultures entails a meeting between two truths. This meeting between two truths leads to changes in relation to the inherent cultural differences, limits or borders. "True understanding not only begins with difference but also requires all horizons to change; neither one's own horizon nor that of the other is left intact" (Barthold, n.d.). New horizons appear as a result of our effort to understand others (Barthold, n.d.)

The fact that one can "access the viewpoint of another from within" his/her own culture is not a "totalitarian effort to defend a mono-culture but a humble admission that one never can access directly the other's perspective" (Barthold, n.d.). In any foreign text there is always a part of a foreign atmosphere that is impossible to reflect in the translation. Fortunately however, translators' attempts are often successful. Looking for the best decision to explain differences between their own cultures and that of foreign cultures translators have the opportunity also to find similarities and link worlds together. The process of translation is usually based on different ways of interpretations of concepts because of which translators' decisions become more subtle, understandable, precise and natural for the translated text, language and culture. In the translation process it is impossible to find better solutions to a problem without a trial-and-error approach.

In the framework of this paper a foreign culture can be presented in the translated text only through the domestication strategy that is based on a comparison between two cultures. The reason is that the translator as well as the target audience can perceive a foreign culture only with the help of comparing it with their own culture, discovering similarities or analogies that exist between them. In other words, comparison in translation is unavoidable because the "language" as the translator's tool "is the site of return, the warm fabric of a memory, and the insisting call from afar, back home" (Minh-ha 2010, 28). The analysis here of examples of translation in the field of travel and tourism shows that translators as cultural mediators need to maintain a balance between the concepts of the foreign and the domestic culture within the text. Similarities are connecting links between the source and the target cultures. These connecting links assist in creating an understanding of cultural differences.

Translation in the field of travel has to solve problems of subjectivity, stereotypes and individual associations which exist in tourists' minds. The main aim of the translators in the field of tourism is to make a foreign culture accessible for readers of a translated text. To make one culture accessible to another does not mean eliminating differing cultural features or creating cultural hegemony, but creating a cultural dialogue between two worlds. This paper suggests looking at the dialogue in translation as one that does not just connect cultures, but creates a platform for presenting differences to the whole world.

References

Baker, Mona. 2011. *In Other Words. A coursebook on translation.* Abingdon, Oxon: Routledge.

Barthold, Lauren Swayne. n.d. "Hans-Georg Gadamer". *Internet Encyclopedia of Philosophy. A Peer-Reviewed Academic Resource,* accessed September 30, 2016, http://www.iep.utm.edu/gadamer/#H3

Bivens, Staci. "Of Russian Origin: Pechka". *RT Russiapedia*, accessed February 13, 2017, http://russiapedia.rt.com/of-russian-origin/pechka/

—. "Of Russian Origin: Prorub". *RT Russiapedia*, accessed February 13, 2017, http://russiapedia.rt.com/of-russian-origin/prorub/

Feifer, Gregory. 2009. "Russian Baths Offer Respite From Bitter Winters". *NPR*, February 26, accessed September 30, 2016, http://www.npr.org/templates/story/story.php?storyId=100699944

Fernandez, Gabriela. "Teach English in Russia & Celebrate Maslenitsa: the Russian Carnival". *International TEFL Academy*, accessed February 13, 2017, https://www.internationalteflacademy.com/blog/bid/204996/teach-english-in-russia-celebrate-maslenitsa-the-russian-carnival

Gentzler, Edwin. 2001. *Contemporary Translation Theories.* Clevedon, Buffalo, Toronto, Sydney: Multilingual Matters.

Hallett, Richard W., and Judith Kaplan-Weinger. 2010. *Official Tourism Websites: A Discourse Analysis Perspective.* Bristol, New York, Canada: Channel View Publications.

Minh-ha, Trinh T. (2010). *Elsewhere, Within Here. Immigration, Refugeeism and the Boundary Event.* New York: Routledge.

Murrell, Kathleen Berton. 2001. *Discovering the Moscow Countryside. A Travel Guide to the Heart of Russia.* London and New York: I.B. Tauris Publishers.

Penn Arts & Sciences. 2016. "Grice's Maxim," accessed September 30, 2016, https://www.sas.upenn.edu/~haroldfs/dravling/grice.html

Pigareva, Olga. 2005. "Of Russian Origin: Skomorokh". *RT Russiapedia,* accessed September 20, 2016, http://russiapedia.rt.com/of-russian-origin/skomorokh/

Pushkova, Darya. "Of Russian Origin: Ushanka". *RT Russiapedia,* accessed February 13, 2017, http://russiapedia.rt.com/of-russian-origin/ushanka/

Pyykkö, Riitta. 2012. "Official and Unofficial Symbols of Russia and their Use in Media". In *Language: Competence—Change—Contact,* edited by Annikki Koskensalo, John Smeds, Rudolf de Cillia, and Angel Huguet, 239—52. Münster: Lit Verlag.

RT Russiapedia. 2005. "Of Russian Origin: Avoska". *RT Russiapedia,* accessed September 30, 2016, http://russiapedia.rt.com/of-russian-origin/ avoska/

Sturge, Kate. 2007. *Representing Others: translation, ethnography, and the museum.* Manchester, UK: St. Jerome Pub.

Teliya, V.N., N. Bragina, E. Oparina and I. Sandomirskays. 1998. "Phraseology as a language of culture: Its role in the representation of a collective memory". In *Phraseology: Theory, Analysis, and Applications,* edited by A.P. Cowie, 55—75. Oxford: Oxford University Press.

Venuti, Lawrence. 2008. *The Translator's Invisibility: A history of translation,* 2nd ed. London: Routledge.

VisitNovgorod. 2014. "Online City Guide of Veliky Novgorod", accessed January 26, 2016, http://visitnovgorod.com/sights/city_guide.html

Vlahov, Sergei, and Sider Florin. 1980. *Neperevodimoye v perevode.* Edited by Vl. Rossels. Moscow: Mezhdunarodnye Otnoshenia.

Part 2:

Perceiving the North—Issues of Identity and Ways of Thinking

CHAPTER FIVE

"A COUNTRY OF UNANSWERED QUESTIONS"—PIERRE BERTON: *THE MYSTERIOUS NORTH*

JANICKE STENSVAAG KAASA

Introduction

To travel in the Canadian north—broadly speaking, the vast area encompassing Yukon, the Northwest Territories, and Nunavut—in the early years after the Second World War meant to travel in a region of rapid and extensive change. For one, the area experienced an increase in military and mining activity, due to its geopolitically and economically important role. This role would continue into the years of the Cold War and is, of course, no less significant today. Moreover, this intensified awareness of the north's strategic and economic potential brought about new understandings of the area as not merely an empty wilderness, but as a place that played a key role in Cold War thinking and as a land of resources and riches to be developed. In this way, the Canadian north, as well as the ideas and meanings of the region, was indeed subject to critical changes during the early postwar years.

One who travelled extensively in the north during this time was the popular Canadian author and journalist Pierre Berton (1920—2004). It is almost impossible to exaggerate Berton's position in Canada: when he passed away in 2004, he had been a well-known figure to Canadians for almost sixty years, and the many obituaries that appeared in the newspapers on the occasion of his death emphasised Berton's unique role in Canadian public life.[1] *CanWest News* reported the loss of "Canada's master storyteller" (Enman 2004, n.p.), and *Globe and Mail* declared that "a voice of Canada is gone" (Martin 2004, n.p.). Even then Prime Minister

---

[1] Obituaries appeared not only in Canadian newspapers, but also in British and U.S. newspapers such as the *Guardian*, *New York Times*, and *Los Angeles Times*.

Paul Martin expressed his sympathies and declared that the passing of Berton "silences a great Canadian voice" (Berton House 2004). Through his long career as a journalist, historian, writer, and public figure, Berton had provided Canadians with stories for nearly six decades and had established himself as what *Saturday Night* referred to as "the official storyteller of the nation" (Cameron 1987, 21).

Many of Berton's stories were about the north, and the Yukon-born author travelled to and wrote about the region throughout his career, although he was based in Toronto for the greater part of his life. He first began writing about the area in the late 1940s working as a reporter for *Vancouver Sun* and *Maclean's* (where he later became managing editor), when he made several trips to various destinations in the Canadian north. During this period Berton published numerous and very successful articles based on his journeys, one of them being "The Mysterious North", which was published in an issue of *Maclean's* in 1954 and which provided a comprehensive overview of the developments in the Canadian north at the time. Both in its title and contents, this article anticipated another significant publication by Berton, namely the autobiographical travel book *The Mysterious North* (1956)[2], which will be the focus of this paper. This was Berton's second book, based on his travels and writings as a journalist from 1947 to 1954, and it covered a wide range of northern topics, such as exploration, geology, history, climate, economy, infrastructure, and tourism.

Although not widely known and read today, *The Mysterious North* was a critically acclaimed best-seller at the time of publication, and it won Berton the 1956 Governor General's Award in the category for creative non-fiction. As such, it marks the very beginning of Berton's remarkable career. Moreover, as A. B. McKillop points out in his biography on Berton, its northern theme also contributed to "the identification of Berton as the voice and chronicler of the North in the public mind" (McKillop 2009, 5—6). The scholarly interest in *The Mysterious North*, though, has been scarce, just as it has been in any of Berton's other writings. And, when Berton's work *is* mentioned, it is most often in passing and, as Geoff Martin has noted, "either in a review or as an introductory hook, a way of gesturing to a popular Canadian perspective before delving into other analyses" (Martin 2012, 51). Rather, the focus has been on Berton's public persona and celebrity status, as in Lorna Irvine's article "The Real Mr. Canada", in which she comments upon some of Berton's writings, but in

---

[2] Berton Pierre, *The Mysterious North* (Toronto: McClelland & Stewart Limited, 1956); all subsequent text references will be cited parenthetically in the text as MN.

which she is concerned first and foremost with Berton as a "representative of Canada" (Irvine 1985, 70), and less with his texts.

This emphasis on Berton's persona is hardly surprising, given his omnipresence in Canadian cultural life, not merely through his numerous writings, but through his extensive work in radio and television (Martin 2012, 58).[3] However, the lack of scholarly interest in his writings is peculiar insofar as his books clearly have played a central role in the fashioning of Berton as the voice and storyteller of the north and even of the nation. For instance, McKillop's point that *The Mysterious North* sparked off Berton as Canada's northern voice surely raises the question of how and why this particular book had such an effect. Yet, few scholars have looked into this matter by way of analysing the text itself. To be fair, Martin has remarked how Berton's placing of himself in the northern landscape in *The Mysterious North* makes a key strategy in the consolidation of his authority as a voice of the north: "What sold 'Pierre Berton', the literary celebrity, was the way he inserted himself into that northern space, asserting the authenticity of his experience and, therefore, the authority of his opinions" (Martin 2012, 54). He does not, however, devote any attention to how this northern space is represented.

Berton's celebrity status, I find, has tended to overshadow the academic interest in his writings in general, and in *The Mysterious North* in particular. To my mind, the popularity of this book and its success in launching Berton as a northern voice in the Canadian public mind prompts a critical study of the text itself and of how and by which strategies the Canadian north is represented. Therefore, my concern in this paper will be with the representation of the Canadian north in *The Mysterious North*. More specifically, I will focus my discussion on the idea of the north as a mysterious place—as "a country of unanswered questions" (MN 9)— which is so clearly emphasised in the title of the book. What, then, is the role of the mysterious in Berton's account of the north?

---

[3] In addition to his many guest appearances, Berton hosted the radio show *Pierre Berton Speaks* and the TV show *The Pierre Berton Hour* (1962), later re-named *The Pierre Berton Show* (1963—1973). Through his work as a radio and TV host, he interviewed famous people like Malcom X, Vladimir Nabokov, Lionel Trilling, Bruce Lee, and Farley Mowat, to name but a few and rather diverse examples. These shows, as well as the use of his full name in the show titles, certainly underline Berton's position and status in the Canadian public mind.

The Canadian North during the Postwar Years

I mentioned in my introduction that *The Mysterious North* was written at a
time when there were significant changes in the Canadian north, due to its
geopolitically and economically important role in the postwar, and later,
Cold War years. Before I begin my discussion of the idea of the
mysterious in Berton's account, I will briefly consider how *The
Mysterious North* also addressed these changes and how it presented the
readers with a wide-ranging scope on the north.

At the time when Berton travelled in the north as a reporter, the
region's strategic role was undeniable: it was considered the place where
the Soviet Union could and *would* strike. For instance, Canadian author
Farley Mowat referred to the area as Canada's "most vulnerable point. It is
our soft belly, and there is no doubt that when the enemy decides to strike,
he will take full advantage of it" (Mowat 1952, 342). The fear of an
imminent attack in the north meant an increase in the US American
presence in the region. For example, US Americans were brought in to
operate the weather and radar stations for the Distant Early Warning
(DEW) Line, commenced in 1954 and set up for early detection of Soviet
air and sea attacks. The area, then, was heavily militarized from the late
1940s onwards, and this fact is an important part of *The Mysterious North*,
in which Berton accounts for the construction and costs of the DEW Line
and describes the life in the U.S. airbases in the Baffin area.

The military demands of the Second World War and the Cold War
motivated several infrastructural developments that made northern
resources more commercially viable on the global market. This was
especially the case for the U.S. market, which looked to the Canadian
north to cover its needs. As a result, private investors from the United
States, together with Canadian companies, initiated and funded large
projects such as the crude oil mining Canol Pipeline Project, commenced
in 1942, and the development of iron ore mines and new railway routes in
order to supply U.S. steel plants. Louis Hamelin has pointed out that the
Second World War's opening up of the north created a "climate of
enthusiasm" (Hamelin 1979, 6) regarding the region. In this excitement,
the government policies became more and more focused on developing the
north through different initiatives. Before the Second World War, the area
had not been a political priority, but the increasingly important role of the
Canadian north in geopolitical, military, and economic issues required a
larger degree of governmental intervention, and the region's social and

economic concerns were being targeted by governmental policies to a much higher degree.[4]

This was indeed a tendency during the government of Prime Minister Louis Stephen St-Laurent (1948—57), but first became an articulated priority with Prime Minister John Diefenbaker's (1957—63) "Northern Vision", which stressed "the opening of the northland by building transportation routes and communication lines, thereby linking northern resources to southern markets" (Bone 2012, 89). In *The Mysterious North*, Berton anticipates this political alertness to the economic prospects of the region and he shares the enthusiasm that Hamelin refers to.[5] Moreover, as McKillop writes, the publication of Berton's book echoed the political interest in the region at the time and "coincided with St. Laurent administration's discovery of northern economic potential, anticipating and perhaps helping shape Diefenbaker's 'northern vision', intent on exploiting this new north and linking it to a distinct Canadian identity" (McKillop 2009, 5). Indeed, the Canadian north, Berton writes, is a reservoir of riches that is waiting to be developed and "to feel the tread of the white man's moccasins" (MN 8). In particular, Berton is interested in the mineral deposits of the region, and he describes attentively different mining projects such as the gold extraction in the Klondike, the iron mining in Ungava and Labrador, and the possible plans for generating hydropower in the Yukon.

Thus, *The Mysterious North* addresses the main postwar developments in the Canadian north; it highlights its strategic and economic potential, and describes the increasing military and industrialized activity at a time when northern affairs were brought into the very foreground of Canadian politics. This concern with the north as a region that is central to Canada's geopolitical role and economy certainly reflects the changing perceptions of the area in the Canadian public, and the tendency to understand the north as something else than mere wasteland and wilderness.

When reading the many reviews of Berton's book, it becomes clear that *The Mysterious North* was applauded for its timely portrayal of the

---

[4] Significantly, the Department of Resources and Development was created in 1950 and was given the responsibility for northern issues—an important response to the new realities of the North. In 1953, the Department would change its name to that of Northern Affairs and National Resources, and this was the first time "northern affairs" was used in a department title.

[5] This notion of the north as a land of resources is further emphasized in some of the visual components in this book. For instance, it is highlighted by the inclusion of a mine shaft on the front cover as well as in the cartographic representations, drawn by Canadian illustrator and artist William Parlane.

changes in the postwar north. For example, *Globe and Mail* considers the account to be "by far the most comprehensive and detailed presentation of the present-day Canadian North" (Deacon 1956, 8) whereas *Saturday Review* reports that "since the economic gravity of Canada and the defense system of America are now tilting northward in Russia's direction Mr. Berton's report is not only a lively record of travel but a timely social document" (Hutchison 1956, 20). As these examples show, the reviewers stressed Berton's interest in the contemporary north and its timely discussion of the area as central to questions of military defense and economy.

However, as I pointed out in my introduction and as the title of the book indicates, Berton's interest lies not only in the north as a land of strategic and economic potential and as the site of military and mining activities: throughout his account he insists upon the idea of the area as a mysterious land, a recurring notion that encompasses several meanings and aspects, some of which I will unpack in the remainder of this paper.

The Spectral North

To Berton, the north is, as I remarked in my introduction, a land of questions that go unanswered, a place of "geological puzzles and scientific mysteries" (MN 9). Even the location of the north causes confusion as "the fact is that nobody can say where 'the north' actually starts" (MN 13). As Berton is aware, this is perhaps a fundamental part of the region's allure, and he writes: "To me, as to most northerners, the country is still an unknown quantity, as elusive as the wolf, howling just beyond the rim of the hills. Perhaps that is why it holds its fascination" (MN 4). In general, Berton is sceptical of the notion that the north is a coherent, definable entity: he dismisses the idea of one single and uniform north and argues instead for an understanding of the region's diversity and incongruity, which takes into account its heterogeneity and contradictions:

> The greatest misconception, of course, is that "the north" is all of a piece from Alaska to Ungava. . . . There is no single *north*, in fact, but several, each quite distinct in climate, topography, economic and social structure. . . . It is, at best, an arbitrary area, distinguished as much by its contradictions as by its uniformities. (MN 12—13)

Berton's emphasis on the *several* norths in this passage testifies to his ambition to expose and disclaim what he considers to be the great misconceptions in the general understanding of the north and to replace these mistaken beliefs with a more comprehensive view of the region that encompasses its diversity.

The Mysterious North considers the north's heterogeneity by accounting for the various districts and the geographic and demographic differences between them, with a particular emphasis on the contemporary strategic and economic developments. Yet, as I have already pointed out, the title of the book implies a rather exclusive focus on the mysterious that does not denote the region as a geopolitical or economic hotspot. What is more, the title refers to the "north" in the singular and thus it does not signal the several norths that Berton accentuates in the beginning of his account. The title, however, does announce the idea that the north is mysterious, which to my mind is dominant throughout Berton's account.

The mysteriousness of the north in Berton's text applies not only to geology, science or geographical boundaries, but connotes several other aspects such as the spectral, the magical and the mythical. This is obvious already in the publisher's text, printed on the book's dust cover:

> The reader is taken across the unmapped tundra, with its ghost-like caribou and mysterious musk-oxen, where the clawmarks of ancient glaciers are still visible. There are other journeys: to a weird "tropical" valley near the Yukon. . . . Here are stories of strange northern phenomena: the fabulous narwhal, with its unicorn's tusk; century-old trees that are three inches tall; wheat sprouting five feet in a month; waterfalls twice as high as Niagara. (MN n.p.)

Here, the reference to the "unmapped tundra" indicates the north as mysterious because it is still unchartered. Similarly, the use of the words "ghost-like", "mysterious", "weird", "strange", and "fabulous" implies a mysterious north, but then in a sense that points more to the spectral, the magical and the mythical.

These aspects of the mysterious are also displayed early on in the main text, when Berton writes about the north:

> Here, where the caribou drift like specters across the tundra, and the aurora sweeps magically across the dark sky, and the sleigh dogs howl in a melancholy choir to the cold moon, it is easy to believe many things. The north is bestrewn with the myths of lost gold mines and tropical valleys and ghostly tribes of devouring Indians. (MN 10)

In this passage, Berton makes use of a vocabulary that contributes to the idea of the north as mysterious by referring to the caribou as specters, to the magical strokes of the aurora and to the many myths of the land. In fact, and as I will elaborate on in the following, the notion of the spectral

plays an important role even earlier on in the account when Berton
introduces himself as the autodiegetic narrator.

In my introduction, I commented on Geoff Martin's observation that
Berton's authority as a northern voice was enabled by how he placed
himself in the northern landscape in *The Mysterious North*. This authority,
Martin argues, derives from the fact that Berton was born and raised in the
north, a fact that he clearly accentuates in the beginning of his account.
This is, no doubt, an important aspect of Berton as a voice of the north. As
McKillop remarks, Berton's northern origins were a great benefit as "it
handed reviewers a ready-made interpretive 'hook' for their pieces: the
subject was in this author's very lifeblood" (McKillop 2010, 299). A quick
glance at the reviews confirms Martin's and McKillop's claim that there is
a tight connection between his authority to speak and his roots in the
region. *Saturday Review*, for example, sees Berton as "equipped by his
birth in Whitehorse, his youth in the dwindling gold town of Dawson City"
(Hutchison 1956, 20), whereas *Globe and Mail* states that "Mr. Berton has
one great advantage over other writers about this vast, various and
dramatic North because he was born in Whitehorse and brought up in
Dawson City" (Deacon 1956, 8). However, what neither Martin, McKillop
nor any of the reviewers mention is how the northern landscape in which
Berton places himself first and foremost is a spectral landscape and how
the spectral characterises his rendering of his childhood and youth
experiences in the Yukon.

In the very beginning of *The Mysterious North*, Berton traces the
origins of his narrative to his origins in the Yukon. He has never, he writes,
"been able to escape the memory of those lonely hills" (MN 3). The north,
he continues, "has dogged my footsteps and I have never quite been quit
of it" (MN 4). Here, Berton renders the north of his childhood years as not
merely an unforgettable, but even *haunting* place. This haunting and
spectral feature of Berton's introduction of himself as the autodiegetic
narrator is further underlined by his reference to the elusive wolf that
dominates his childhood memories of the north:

> In the winter nights . . . when the ghostly bars of the northern lights shifted
> across the black sky, we would sometimes hear the chill call of the wolf,
> drifting down from the wilderness behind us. It is an eerie sound, plaintive,
> mournful, mysterious. . . . If the north has a theme song, it is this haunting
> cry, which seems to echo all the loneliness and the wonder of the land at
> the top of the continent. When I was a small boy, it used to fascinate and
> terrify me, perhaps because in all my years in the north I never actually
> saw a wolf alive. To me he was only a footprint in the snow and a sound in
> the night, an unseen creature who lurked in the shadow of the nameless
> hills. (MN 3–4)

In this passage, Berton's association of the north with the mysterious and the spectral in particular is accentuated by the wolf's eerie and haunting cry as well as by the fact that the wolf remains an unseen creature and thus, perhaps, remains a mystery.

Just like his northern origins, Berton's extensive travel experiences in the north later in life do not seem to make the mysteriousness of the north any smaller to him. Rather, the opposite seems to be the case when Berton writes that "the more I see of the country, the less I feel I know about it" (MN 4). The north, he goes on some pages later, remains a place that "continues to elude us" (MN 8). Already from the very beginning, then, and inseparable from Berton's placing of himself in the northern landscape, the north is represented as mysterious insofar as it is an elusive, spectral and even threatening place.

In his emphasis on the Canadian north as mysterious in the sense that I have discussed above, Berton draws on a northern topos that is recurrent in so much of the writing about the north and the Arctic. For one, the threatening and almost gothic characterisation of the north in Berton's introduction of himself as a northerner calls to mind the dark and hostile Arctic of Mary Shelley's *Frankenstein* (1818). Moreover, the fact that the wolf's chilling calls both fascinate and terrify Berton suggests a sublime experience of the north, which most certainly is an important feature in *Frankenstein* as well as in several expedition accounts from the north. As Chauncey C. Loomis has noted in his article "The Arctic Sublime", there is in the cultural history of the Arctic a notion of the place as "vaster, more mysterious, and more terrible than elsewhere on the globe—a region in which natural phenomena could take strange, almost supernatural forms, sometimes stunningly beautiful, sometimes terrifying, often both" (Loomis 1977, 96). Certain elements from Loomis' description do indeed fit Berton's portrayal of his childhood north as symbolized by the elusive wolf: here too, the north is strange and almost supernatural; here too, it is both beautiful and terrifying.

Another World, Another Time

Thus far my discussion of the notion of the mysterious north in Berton's account has been concerned with the spectral north. Another aspect of the mysterious in Berton's text, which I will comment on in the following and which certainly is closely linked to the idea of the north as a spectral and haunting place, concerns the north as a land where myths and legends are abundant. Throughout his account, Berton refers to northern myths and legends such as the McLeod brothers' death in "Headless Valley", which, he writes, has "long since become a northern fable" (MN 63). He refers also to the so-called Mad Trapper, who "has become one of the north's most indestructible legends" (MN 252).[6] However, the north in Berton's account is not merely the backdrop against which these myths and legends may unfold: it is itself a mythical and legendary land.

Berton underlines this mythical character of the north throughout his account. For example, when flying over the Nahanni area, he refers to the landscape below him as a "northern never-never land" (MN 25). Later in the account, when taking the Quebec North Shore and Labrador railway towards the iron plateau, he describes how he has entered "an unearthly world, half fairyland, half purgatory" (MN 221). Then, when he soars over the Precambrian shield, he makes a similar reference and sums up the scene in the following way: "There it lay below us, the spine of Canada . . . as desolate and empty-looking as a dead planet in science fiction" (MN 275). In a final example, Berton has returned to his home in Toronto after a visit to Pond Inlet, where three "unicorn" tusks of the narwhale at the trading post "seemed to spring right from a Tenniel illustration in Lewis Carroll" (MN 202), and comments on how the north and the people living there "seemed as distant as the mountains of the moon" (MN 204). Here, Berton continues to describe the north in terms that connote both the threatening and the supernatural, which I discussed above.

Moreover, in these examples, the north is portrayed as a distant and remote area that is desolate, empty and dead. For one, this view on the region somewhat contradicts Berton's emphasis elsewhere in the account, where the north is promoted as a region of resources waiting to be developed—an understanding that evidently is based on the very assumption that the region is *not* empty or dead. Second, and more relevant to the context of the mysterious, these references insist on the idea of the north as a land that is itself mythical and legendary, which, in turn, implies an imaginary north: to me, Berton's representation of the north as an unearthly and fairy-like "never-never land" and his association of the Precambrian shield with a science-fiction planet facilitate an understanding of the north as an unearthly and even unreal and imaginary place. It becomes, in Peter Davidson's term, a "northern otherworld"

---

[6] The unidentified Mad Trapper is known only by his pseudonym Albert Johnson. He died in the Yukon after the largest manhunt in Canada's history when he, after having killed one RCMP officer and harmed two others, was shot dead in the winter of 1932. Attempts are still being made to this day to find out his true identity. For a fictionalized account of the story, see Rudy Wiebe's *The Mad Trapper* (1980).

(Davidson 2005, 32). As such, the idea of the mysterious north in Berton's account involves the idea of *another world* entirely.

This otherworldly aspect of Berton's representation of the Canadian north is further emphasised by the notion of the north as a place where time has stood still. I have already commented upon how Berton underlines the region's distance and, evidently, the idea of the north as another world is due to the geographical remoteness of the north from the Canadian south—and vice versa. Yet, the distance in Berton's account is also of a temporal character, and he repeatedly portrays the north as an unchanged land of the past, where time has stood still. As such, the emphasis on the geographical remoteness of the region may be read as a representational strategy that insists on its temporal distance. As Neil Rennie has remarked: "To discover a place remote in space—remote, that is, from civilized culture—was to discover a place apparently remote in time, a place with a 'primitive' culture, primal, original, like the beginning of the world" (Rennie 1995, 1). In a similar fashion, Carl Thompson has identified the "frequent conflation of geographical and temporal distance in many Western travelogues", in which the travellers "present themselves as going back in time, encountering 'Stone Age', 'Bronze Age' or 'medieval' cultures that are assumed to have remained unchanged for centuries" (Thompson 2011, 147).[7] This is very much the case in Berton's account, in which the remoteness of the region applies not merely to its geographical location, but also to its distance in historical time. As such, and as I will explore further in what follows, the north that Berton portrays remains "stuck in an earlier historical phase" (Thompson 2011, 147), which makes the north no less mysterious.

There are several examples of how Berton renders the Canadian north as a place remote in time. The muskox, for instance, is described as the

---

[7] As Thompson makes clear, he here draws on anthropologist Johannes Fabian's famous discussion of the "denial of coevalness", which he describes as "a persistent and systematic tendency to place the referent(s) of anthropology in a Time other than the present of the producer of anthropological discourse" (Fabian 1983, 31). Although Fabian is concerned with such denial of coevalness in anthropological discourse, the concept has become central to travel writing theory, as exemplified by Thompson's work. This is especially the case in studies of "othering" in colonial travel books, where the travellers often take it for granted that only they and their countrymen are truly modern and of the present, whereas the "others", meaning the indigenous peoples of the land the travellers are visiting, are not. Fabian's concept of the "denial of coevalness" is also relevant to Berton's representation of the north, and then to his representation of the indigenous peoples living in the Canadian north in particular. It does not, however, fit the scope of this paper.

"most mysterious" of the creatures there and as "a leftover from a forgotten era" (MN 341). The emphasis on the north as unchanged land that is lingering in the past, though, is especially striking in his descriptions from above as he flies over the landscape. Here, he refers to how "the Ice Age was still with us, here among these alpine pinnacles" (MN 47), and remarks that "the land below us now seemed more ancient than anything I had yet seen" (MN 208). Likewise, when flying over the Barren lands, he comments on how "no man can fail to be moved by this empty country which has changed not a whit in twenty centuries" (MN 331). In general, Berton's account of the north repeatedly places the land in a primeval setting, for example when he travels by car on the Alaska Highway, which recently has opened "to unrestricted tourist travel" (MN 141), and comments on how the landscape, with the exception of the highway, appears prehistoric:

> The whole country had a prehistoric look to it. Except for the thin highway snaking between the granite spires, the land was unmarred by human corrosion. The mountains seemed as raw and new as they were when the claws of the cordilleran icecaps gouged them into their present shapes. (MN 156)

Moreover, towards the end of his account, Berton writes of the Barren lands that "most of our great Arctic explorers have been haunted by this prehistoric land, though not all of them have understood it" (MN 330). Here, Berton again refers to the north as a haunting land—and thus links his own childhood experiences of the land to those of the explorers. In the same way, he connects his and the explorers' experience of the land in their joint lack of comprehension of the land. Most important here, though, is how the north is a prehistoric land that seems to be prior to and free, or at least almost free, from human intervention.

Evidently, these references to the land as prehistoric are an important part of Berton's notion of the Canadian north as a place remote from preceding modernisation and so-called civilization. However, I should mention that there are parts of the north that are *not* depicted as prehistoric, but as belonging to the present day. These are first and foremost places of economic and military activity, which Berton is so interested in. When Berton describes his arrival or departure from these places and his moving in between them, he stresses how he seems to travel in time. Towards the end of his account, for example, Berton refers to his flight home as heading back "toward civilization" and "to the land of traffic lights and parking meters" (MN 344). And, earlier in his account, he describes his arrival at the Frobisher Bay airbase as moving into the present time, where, stepping out of the aircraft, "after crossing a thousand miles of dead and empty land, we stepped out into the twentieth century" (MN 210). When he leaves the airbase, the movement in historical time is reversed, and Berton feels as if he is not merely leaving the airbase, but the twentieth century altogether:

> I had one final glimpse of Frobisher Bay, with its huge machines and its men scurrying against time, and then once again we were drifting over the bleak expanse of the iron country. Now the sense of urgency and pressure left us. For the next five hours we left the twentieth century behind and seemed to hang suspended over forests primeval and lands forlorn. (MN 218)

Moreover, when describing the DEW line construction site on Baffin Island, Berton writes: "The great island had come alive with planes, machines, and men. The feeling of *timelessness* had vanished and a sense of urgency now prevailed. Bulldozers had replaced Eskimo komatiks, and Coca-Cola flowed like ice water" (MN 205, emphasis added). As these passages suggest, there *are* parts of the Canadian north that are of the twentieth century. What these areas have in common and what makes them of the present time, Berton seems to reason, is the presence of men and machines and of military activity in particular. Thus, the modernised north exists alongside, and is seemingly separated from the prehistoric and perhaps more mysterious North.

The notion of the mysterious, however, applies not merely to the prehistoric: objects and people of Berton's time are also rendered through a vocabulary that draws on the mythical. For instance, the gold dredge by the Klondike River is referred to as "A Mechanical Monster" that "Chews Up the Storied Klondike" (MN n.p.), and is thus turned into a mythical and threatening figure in the Klondike landscape. Likewise, in his writing of the mining engineer Thayer Lindsley, Berton describes him as "another northern legend, as mysterious as the country that has made him powerful" (MN 107). As such, the notion of the mysterious is reserved not only for the seemingly prehistoric landscapes of the north, which would perhaps lend themselves more easily to mythologizing, but it enters into the descriptions of the mechanical and man-made interventions that shape the land. In this way, the notion of the mysterious enters into the portrayal of contemporary developments in the region.

Another strategy by which Berton depicts the north as a land where time has stood still is by his frequent references to exploration history and to early explorers. The north, Berton writes, "remains as it was in Leif Ericsson's time, a secret land of mystery, enigma, and legend" (MN 8).

The understanding of the region as a land that remains in the past seems to be true for many of Berton's experiences in the North, which he often describes as being the same as when the explorers first laid their eyes on the land. One example is when Berton and his travel companions arrive at the Finlay Forks settlement, and he writes of the place that it remains largely the same and "as aboriginal" (MN 40) as when Scottish explorer Alexander Mackenzie saw it for the first time in 1793. And when flying over the southern tips of Baffin Island Berton observes, with reference to English explorer Martin Frobisher's landing in 1576, that "most of Baffin remains much as it was when the first white men sailed up these waters" (MN 210), and that "we ourselves might have been looking at the island through Elizabethan eyes, so little had this section of it changed over the centuries" (MN 185). Likewise, the districts of Keewatin and Franklin are portrayed as almost untouched from how they must have appeared to the English explorer Henry Hudson in the early 1600s:

> Indeed, save for a handful of trading settlements, it has not changed appreciably since the bleak summer in 1611 when Henry Hudson's starving and diseased crew cast him adrift without food or water in a tossing shallop on the leaden surface of the bay that now bears his name. (MN 177)

The numerous references to the history of exploration in the land that later would become known as Canada permeate throughout Berton's account, and his experience of the landscape is indeed shaped by his readings of these earlier explorers' texts: he seems to read the landscape not merely through his own experience of it, but also through these prior accounts of the region. As such, Berton's experience, understanding and rendering of the landscape in his account is conditioned by the frameworks and expectations set by these earlier writings.

Berton also includes more recent figures from the history of exploration, such as Vilhjalmur Stefansson, Roald Amundsen and Warburton Pike. For example, he quotes the latter and observes how his description of the tundra is still valid for the landscape that meets Berton: "Those words were written over sixty years ago, but the land is exactly as it was when Pike crossed the tundra. With the exceptions noted, nothing has changed, for this is a land that knows neither erosion by the elements nor encroachment by civilization" (MN 329). In yet another example, the unchanged character of the north is highlighted with reference to explorers following in each other's tracks:

The cart tracks left on the tundra on Melville Island by Sir Edward Parry in 1820 were visible to Leopold M'Clintock, who followed his trail thirty-three years later. Hardly a speck of moss had grown over them. It was as if Parry himself were only a few miles away, instead of a generation or more. (MN 329)

The visibility of Parry's cart tracks in this passage would of course be due to circumstances such as permafrost and the short growing seasons, which do not allow the tundra to recover quickly from interference. Yet, in a passage like this, Berton pulls both Parry and M'Clintock into his own present and brings them into physical proximity with his own geographical position. Temporal distance is turned into local proximity, and the tundra remains as it was in the 1820s.

Berton's numerous references to earlier explorations and travels serve to underline that the land has not changed appreciably. What is more, they imply that the remoteness of the land concerns not only its geographical, but also its temporal distance. In this way, travelling north in Berton's account involves travelling back in time: going north, you venture into another world and another time.

Concluding Remarks

This paper has explored various aspects of the notion of the mysterious in Berton's account *The Mysterious North*. The most obvious way in which this idea of the mysterious north is developed is through Berton's emphasis on the area as a land still unmapped. As unchartered land it is still, and will perhaps continue to be, "a country of unanswered questions" (MN 9). However, as I have argued there are several other connotations of the mysterious that are at play in Berton's text. For one, his self-representation employs a rhetoric that renders the north a spectral place and a haunting experience: the chilling calls of the elusive wolf become the dominant image of his childhood memories in the Yukon. Moreover, the north is highlighted as a mythical and legendary land, to the extent that it becomes unreal. Moreover, as a marvellous and enigmatic place, likely to be taken from a science fiction narrative, it becomes not merely imaginary, but also another world entirely. This otherworldliness, my discussion has shown, applies also to time: again and again, parts of the north are represented as prehistoric places where time has stood still. Yet, the region's contemporary postwar developments are also rendered mysterious. Indeed, in a prescient passage, Berton even remarks on how "the north has been slowly and mysteriously warming up" (MN 328). However, as the link between climate changes and human CO_2 emissions was not yet developed at the time, the warming up of the north must according to Berton "be numbered among the northern mysteries" (MN 329). As the title of his book implies, the north in Berton's account remains mysterious: it remains a land of unanswered questions despite his ambitions to and efforts in answering them: it is, and will continue to be a place of "secrets; secrets everywhere" (Wiebe 1989, 44), as Rudy Wiebe has noted in his contemplation on the Arctic.

Returning to the postwar context that I introduced in the beginning of this paper, it is somewhat peculiar that the idea of the mysterious plays such an important part of Berton's account. His emphasis on the economic and strategic developments of the land, and his understanding of the north as a reservoir of riches and a strategically important spot, suggest a view of the area that does not leave much room for the mysterious. Rather, it connotes an attitude to the land as a place to be mapped, extracted, gained, put into service. Moreover, the fact that Berton places himself in a mysterious and spectral landscape from the very beginning of his account further adds to the notion that the north resists full disclosure, even to those who are northerners. As he writes early on in the travel book:

> There is a saying that after five years in the north every man is an expert; after ten years, a novice. No man can hope or expect to absorb it all in a lifetime, and fifteen generations of explorers, whalers, fur traders, missionaries, scientists, policemen, trappers, prospectors, adventurers, and tourists have failed to solve its riddles. (MN 4)

To me, Berton's recognition of and emphasis on the mysteriousness of the Canadian north constitute a central part in the book's success. It is, I believe, also important to the understanding of the consolidation of Berton as *the* northern voice. By keeping the north in the realm of the mysterious Berton draws on familiar ideas of an unfamiliar region: he renders the north as a spectral, threatening, and sublime space, and thus he evokes some of the key topoi in the cultural history of the north. In this way, he draws on the very ideas that increase the area's appeal: to deprive the north of its mysteriousness would mean to deprive it of its allure. Moreover, in a time of postwar change, where the roles and the meanings of the north are in rapid transition, the prominence given to the mysterious may be read as an effort to maintain the familiar and longstanding understanding of the north as a place with which man can never be acquainted. As such, the riddles of the north will, and should, never be solved.

References

Berton House Writers' Retreat. 2004. "Statement by Prime Minister Paul Martin on the death of Pierre Berton", accessed September 3, 2016, http://www.bertonhouse.ca/pierre.html

Berton, Pierre. 1956. *The Mysterious North*. Toronto: McClelland & Stewart Limited.

Bone, Robert M. 2012 [1992]. *The Canadian North: Issues and Challenges*. 4th ed. Don Mills, ON: Oxford University Press.

Cameron, Elspeth. 1987. "Once Upon a Time". *Saturday Night*, Aug., 19—30.

Davidson, Peter. 2005. *The Idea of North*. London: Reaktion Books.

Deacon, William Arthur. 1956. "'The Tundra Rolled On Majestic in Its Monotony'". *The Globe and Mail*, March 3, 8.

Enman, Charles. 2004. "Canada's Master Storyteller Never Expected to Live so Long". *CanWest News*, Dec. 1, n.p.

Fabian, Johannes. 1983. *Time and the Other. How Anthropology Makes its Object*. New York: Columbia University Press.

Hamelin, Louis-Edmond. 1979 [1975]. *Canadian Nordicity: It's Your North, Too*. Translated by William Barr. Montreal: Harvest House.

Hutchison, Bruce. 1956. "From the Yukon to Ungava". *The Saturday Review*, March 10, 20.

Irvine, Lorna. 1985. "The Real Mr. Canada". *Canadian Literature*. Winter, 68—79.

Loomis, Chauncey C. 1977. "The Arctic Sublime". In *Nature and the Victorian Imagination*, edited by U.C. Knoepflmacher and G.B. Tennyson, 95—112. Berkeley: University of California Press.

Martin, Geoff. 2012. "Pierre Berton, Celebrity, and the Economics of Authenticity". *Canadian Literature*. Spring, No. 212, 50—66.

Martin, Sandra. 2004. "A Voice of Canada is Gone as Pierre Berton Dies at 84". *The Globe and Mail*, Dec. 1, n.p.

McKillop, A. B. 2009. "Books, Brands, and Berton". *Underhill Review*, Fall, 1—23.

—. 2010 [2008]. *Pierre Berton: A Biography*. Toronto: Emblem, McClelland & Stewart.

Mowat, Farley. 1952. *People of the Deer*. Boston: Little, Brown & Company.

Rennie, Neil. 1995. *Far-Fetched Facts. The Literature of Travel and the Idea of the South Seas*. Oxford: Clarendon Press.

Thompson, Carl. 2011. *Travel Writing*. London and New York: Routledge.

Wiebe, Rudy. 1989. *Playing Dead. A Contemplation Concerning the Arctic*. Edmonton: NeWest.

CHAPTER SIX

"SIKORSKI'S TOURISTS" AND THEIR CONFRONTATION WITH THE "ICY NORTH"

JOANNA WITKOWSKA

"Sikorski's tourists" were Polish army members who, after the fall of their country in the so-called September campaign of 1939 (the Polish War of Defence), which started on 1st September with the German bombardment of Westerplatte garrison in Gdańsk, forced their way through to their Western allies to continue their participation in World War II and win Poland its freedom.[1] General Władysław Sikorski was the Prime Minister of the Polish government in exile formed in France and then, after its surrender, moved to London. Evacuation of the Polish military, first to France, which Witold Urbanowicz, one of the future Polish fighter aces and Squadron Leader of the famous 303 Squadron called "the country of our dreams", and later north to Britain, called "Last Hope Island", was extremely difficult because the direct way via Germany was out of the question. Possible routes from Poland to allied countries included venturing south—via Romania and the Black Sea ports to the Mediterranean, Lebanon and Egypt or through Slovakia and Hungary to Yugoslavia, Greece and Italy. The possible route north was via Lithuania/Latvia and the Baltic Sea, then Sweden, Denmark, the Netherlands and Belgium. Any routes east were through ports in Soviet Russia. There were also those who reached France through deserts in central Asia (Karakum Desert), Iran and North Africa (Olson and Cloud 2004, 76, 79—81, 90—91). In the end about 200,000 of these Poles reached France. The German minister of propaganda in Adolf Hitler's government, Joseph Goebbels, in one of the radio

---

[1] Since September 17th Poles had to confront another enemy because the Soviet Union attacked Poland from the east. The battle for the capital city of Warsaw lasted from September 8th till September 27th. Sporadic fights continued until the spring of 1940.

broadcasts disparagingly referred to them as "Sikorski's tourists" (http://www.zapisanewkronikach.pl/2014/01/turysci-sikorskiego.html).

This "tourism" continued throughout the war. Polish Armed Forces fought under British command in all theatres of the conflict: in Norway (the Battle of Narvik, April 1940), in the Battle for France (May—June 1940) and the Battle of Britain (July—October 1940). In 1944 and 1945 the I Polish Corps went into combat in France, Belgium, the Netherlands and Germany; in 1941/1942 the Polish Independent Carpathian Rifle Brigade fought in North Africa. The latter, together with the Polish Army formed in the USSR, became the II Polish Corps which fought in Italy under General Władysław Anders from December 1943 (https://ww2.pl/polish-armed-forces-in-the-west/). The post-World War II period saw the publication of many war recollections. I would like to argue in this paper that these recollections are as much war accounts as they are travel accounts and, by implication, that Poles took part in the war not only in their capacity as army members but also as travellers displaying the features of tourists. Since Poles travelled north, the question about the role of the north as a concept in their perceptions of the British other will be raised when analysing Polish-British encounters.

Veterans' recollections are often appreciated for their military perspective. The authors are rightly honoured as those who sacrificed their lives fighting for their nation's cause. Their testimony is all the more valuable since they speak from the position of eyewitnesses of history, and recollections add credibility to their experiences. However, it is the non-military moments of veterans' wartime existence which counterbalanced, even if insufficiently, the horrors of combat. For psychological wellbeing and battlefield efficiency, the identity of a soldier had to be, at times, hidden, and prominence to peacetime identities given instead. Constantly on the move and thus exposed to the kaleidoscope of changing foreign surroundings that triggered their (careful) attention like that of newcomers, Polish combatants, as if it were natural, became involved in the observation of the British other, assuming their travellers' identities. The latter comes as no surprise since recollections written by "Sikorski's tourists" belong to military memoirs which, as noted by university professor and war veteran Samuel Hynes, reveal the characteristics of autobiography, history, but also travel writing (McNaylor 2003, 795). After all, if travelling is about going from one place to another then it is part and parcel of soldiers' lives. As Gavin Daly points out, the universality of this relationship has been signalled already in Homer's *Odyssey* and yet it was long neglected: "They [soldiers] are rarely considered as travellers, and their writings are rarely appreciated as travel narratives. Only in recent years has this begun to change with respect to soldiers of the French Revolutionary-Napoleonic Wars" (Daly 2013, 9). Consequently, the authority of the words they spoke on the pages of their recollections sprang not only from their role of a combatant but also of a traveller/tourist (Ibid.).

For the sake of terminological exactitude it should be mentioned that after the development of mass tourism in the 19th century, the traveller/tourist distinction appeared. Before this these words were almost synonymous (Smethurst 2003, 1186). Thus, a tourist started to be perceived as a product of the leisure industry, which serves those willing to travel effortlessly by suggesting places worth seeing and providing all facilities, including accommodation and transportation. Client satisfaction is the primary aim, but so is commercial profit, hence the emphasis on the commodification of all elements of the sale process. In contrast, travellers are supposed to be more independent and curious minds. Unguided by a tourist company, they put more effort in their travelling adventure and take all responsibility for the danger it may pose. Since travellers aim to acquire knowledge, they also have a drive for sharing their experience with others (Jasiakiewicz 2010, 28—29). Paul Fussell says:

> [A tourist] is not self-directed but externally directed. You go not where you want to go but where the industry has decreed that you shall go. Tourism soothes you by comfort and familiarity and shields you from the shocks of novelty and oddity. It confirms your prior view of the world instead of shaking it up. Tourism requires that you see conventional things, and that you see them in a conventional way. (Fussell 1987, 651)

Distancing himself from a moral delineation between a tourist and a traveller, Richard White points to the cultural outlook a tourist takes in his role of a spectator. The willingness to see differentiates him/her from those who come to places for other purposes—e.g. professional, military or those whose status lifts the barrier between the observer and the observed (the host country), e.g. assimilated immigrants. Thus, what may seem to be a tourist's weak point becomes their advantage:

> The point of view is always an outsider's. If it were not, there would, in a sense, be nothing to observe. And this is the point of course: the limitation of the tourist's vision is also its strength because the tourist looks on from outside, but always with something to compare, always able to see through the pretensions of a particular time and place. (White 1997, 117—118)

Several authors have acknowledged the role of tourists in combatants referring to them as "military tourists" (Leighton 2013, 50), "tourists in uniform" (Struk 2011, 52) or "tourists with guns and pens" (Cox 2005, 165). In "Introduction to the 1989 Edition" of *The Tourist. A New Theory of the Leisure Class* the American sociologist Dean MacCannell states: "What is an expeditionary force without guns? Tourists" (MacCannell 1999, xxiv). In what follows, in reference to veterans, various travel-related terms will be used interchangeably including: "tourists", "travellers", "visitors" and "sojourners". Apart from linguistic variety, it is to emphasise the condition of movement, their status as foreigners in British culture and the "traveller's mind" (their already mentioned "view from the outside"). Reservation must be made though, that the Polish military were not tourists or globetrotters in the literal or peacetime meaning of the words, even though they assumed the roles of such when circumstances allowed for it. First of all, it was the war conditions that dictated the time and the direction of their movements. However, the war triggered the latter. As Cox writes about an American Civil War soldier, "[he] does not travel with complete freedom. Still, travel he does" (2005, 173). Breaks from warfare, in a way, enforced sightseeing in the situation when leave could not be spent with their families (left behind in Poland). Other forms of entertainment were scarce or unattractive, and the need to kill time was pressing. The aim of the movement was also different than in peacetime. It was not to see places (Leighton 2013, 119). However, it did not mean that soldiers were insensitive to the tourist tradition and devoid of curiosity about the world (Ibid.). All the more so as for many it was their first time abroad and "travel too was a big attraction" (Ibid., 120). Still, leisure experienced during travel in the moments of redeployment, waiting for combat, recuperation and already mentioned leave, was not tantamount, psychologically or sociologically speaking either, to vacation days, that is "war was [not] simply a kind of holiday" (Ibid., 125). Suffering, death and destruction were day-to-day occurrences, which intruded on the experience of the other. In this context, the inconvenience resulting from poor accommodation in unfriendly climates (for instance tents and barracks in cold and rainy Scotland) were a minor issue, but then it still contrasted with the comfortable hotels booked by tourists. Finally, Daly (2013, 214—215) emphasises combatants' special position among the local population. Billeted in British homes or invited there as guests, singled out by their uniforms and cheered as the country's defenders, they could mingle with various strata of society, thus being far from anonymous tourists and tourists' coincidental relations with the landscapes and peoples they visited. Unpredictable circumstances often forced them to move out of their comfort zones. Following the tourist-traveller dichotomy they would then swing towards the traveller role. The instinct of a pedagogue manifesting itself in the need to preserve the memories for posterity would reveal the traveller in them too (Fussell 1987, 15). Together with the perspective of an outsider and a curious attitude towards observed reality, they would produce war recollections which, as mentioned before, bore the features of travel literature. Many sources note that the latter "has taken on a bewildering multiplicity of forms and functions" (Speake 2003, vii), hence the difficulty to give one comprehensive definition. Wojciech Jasiakiewicz underlines the terminological variety of the genre: "Dictionaries of literary terms and internet sources interchangeably use such concepts as travel writing, travelogues, travel literature or literature of travel and exploration" (2010, 16).

If the reason for travel, as reflected in such literature, is to escape "from the construction of the daily, the job, the boss, the parents" and/or "the pleasure of learning new things" (Fussell 1987, 13) then veterans' writing did not meet these requirements. However, regularly recalled features of travel literature which comprise the object of interest of travel writers, do allow considering of Polish authors' war recollections as part of the genre, defined as: "a non-fictional narrative written in the first person singular (or plural), describing a journey—less often a period of residence in a foreign country, full of observations of landscapes encountered, their geography, flora and fauna, human inhabitants, their lifestyles, history, and social customs" (Microsoft (R) Encarta 1993—1996, in: Jasiakiewicz 2010, 17).

Going north became the call of the day for those of "Sikorski's tourists" for whom Britain became their last point of destination and wartime home from which they continued their armed struggle with their British brothers in arms. As mentioned in the beginning, to reach Albion Poles travelled north from continental Europe—for instance when they left Poland via the Baltic and Scandinavian states, and also when we take into consideration France as their point of departure. Reaching France in itself required movement north for those who travelled from outside Europe—Northern Africa or the Middle East. Finally, when in Britain, Poles moved north to their assigned military bases, with some going as far as Scotland. For the purpose of further analysis of Polish-British relations and of drawing ideational boundaries to their presentation, it is worthwhile to define the role of "the north" in the general audience's imagination and its place in German ideology.

The meaning of the north goes far beyond a mere point of indicating direction or location. Peter Davidson, as a point of departure in *The Idea of North* makes the observation, repeated several times on the pages of his book, that "everyone carries their own idea of North within them" (2005, 8, 9, 11). As he explains, this differentiation oscillates, among others, along political, geographical and historical lines and penetrates countries as well as people in general, their cultural output and individual minds. Quite reflective of this is the expression "true north", which apart from referring to "the direction towards the top of the earth along an imaginary line at an angle of 90 degrees to the equator" (http://dictionary.cambridge.org/dictionary/english/true-north), may have a personal, as if spiritual, point of reference which helps to find a life balance: "there exists somewhere the place that is the absolute of the north, the north in essence, northness in concentration and purity" (Davidson 2005, 11).

"North" is, often from Antiquity, associated with difficult weather conditions: rain, wind, cold, snow, darkness and the Arctic landscape, but can also be gendered as in the case of the Snow Queen and the Ice Witch (Ibid., 9).[2] On the mental level it represents melancholy, remoteness, isolation and stillness, whereas for those willing to search for the self the north may also offer purification, refuge and truth (Davidson 2005). The fascination among the British writers of the 1930s with travelling north (theme) stemmed from the idea of "admirable heroic effort" and the "moral worth" related to it, as well as the idea of moving upwards and thus being "nearer to the top of the world" (Cunningham 1988, 166). Canadian discourses present the country's metaphorical north as wilderness, freedom, mystery, escape and, similarly to British notions, as challenge. However, at the same time, the north assumes ideological meanings which are open for nationalistic discourses, the concept of national identity, unity and the place of the indigenous population (Hulan 2002). Finally, in European mythology, north is Nordic, and the latter relates to the Nordic race. In the context of World War II these references to Nordic concepts acquired a particular, negative meaning, since the Nazis distorted them up to the point of creating a racist ideology, claiming the Nordic race to be superior. Norse mythology had an influence on Hitler and his entourage. The German dictator appreciated the Nordic god of war, Wotan—also called Odin or Woden—and the military plan against the Soviet Union was codenamed Operation Wotan. If Poles had known about these sympathies then the north, and/or going north, should have occurred to them as something disastrous because it had been the northern race that

---

[2] More on gendered aspects of the concept of North can be found in e.g. the representation of Canadian North in Renée Hulan's *Northern Experience and the Myths of Canadian Culture* (Montreal & Kingston, London, Ithaca: McGill-Queen's University Press, 2002).

had invaded their country, in the name of the superior race closely associated with the north. The analysis of the selected Polish war memoirs, referred to later in the paper, does not confirm such associations though. The Slavs relied on more conventional concepts. Britain was associated with geographical north and related to it adverse weather conditions which could impact on physical as well as mental wellbeing of the Polish sojourners. As far as the British hosts are concerned, Poles projected on them stereotypical images of cold Britons.

On the pages of recollections, Scotland in particular became infamous for its unwelcoming aura. Combatant Antoni Wasilewski puts the blame for this on the country's location. Scotland, after all, is for him "remote and cold" and "subarctic" (1978, 150, 206). On the day of his excursion to the city of Elgin he writes: "We are hurtling towards 'the Arctic Circle', northwards, to Elgin!"[3] (Ibid., 235). The cold, the rain, the wind and the damp veterans complained about when in Scotland were all the more vexing as they were often accommodated in quite primitive conditions with no access to basic facilities or hot water. Health concerns occupied the men. They suffered from common cold and flu and the climate activated rheumatic diseases: "It's raining as if through a sieve. Interesting that the rain does not get tired! . . . This is horrible! The damp drives me mad. Everything wet—even my knee suffers from it" (Ibid., 46). References to Poland were frequent, which might have been a strategy to deal with what was new. Military tourists "domesticated" the British weather by describing it through the prism of what they were familiar with. Thus strong Scottish winds were compared to "halny"—the foehn wind characteristic for the Tatra mountains in southern Poland (and Slovakia), and Scottish autumn winds were said to be "equally strong and maybe more howling" than in Poland (Żegota-Januszajtis 2006, 33).

Atmospheric conditions influenced, and at the same time reflected, mental states. By triggering the mind to drift towards Poland, the weather activated homesickness: "Although it is still raining, my thoughts are wondering round Kraków. The sun must be shining there" (Wasilewski 1978, 53). In a somewhat philosophical fashion, Ksawery Pruszyński contemplated the lack of emotional warmth, characteristic of familial relations, to compensate for the inhospitability of foreign nature: "Damp nights and rainy days are dangerous not for rifle barrels only. Souls get rusty, too, without the ointment of good news from home, of a kind word, of family warmth and friendly feeling" (2010, 18). The lack of sunlight deepened the experience of war losses and fostered melancholic states

---

[3] All translations of Polish texts are mine [Joanna Witkowska].

which, even if "transitory" in Burton's sense, are inherent to our human existence. In the longer run this could be conducive to becoming a "habit", and thus turning into a clinical condition (Burton 2004).

On the more metaphorical level, northerness became a quality attributed to the British nature and thus entered the platform of Polish-British interpersonal relationships. In its variety it could manifest itself in the distance, which some Britons apparently displayed towards Poles. Pilot Stefan Łaszkiewicz praised earlier cooperation with the French ally, portrayed by him as kind, obliging and approachable (1982, 272). "Nobody turned up their nose there. Nobody looked at us as werewolves", confirmed his colleague, Gomuliński, only to conclude complaining about their new, British colleagues: "And here, dammit, icy North" (Ibid.).

Selected for the purpose of the paper, war accounts show that Poles had brought with them to Albion many, often stereotypical, preconceptions about its inhabitants. The reason for this might be historical. Poles and Britons never had close relationships; it was France that was Poland's natural ally. Although this is not to say that there were no Polish-British relationships at all, they were just too insignificant for common Poles to enable them to form their own, first hand, opinions of the Islanders. The language barrier would not make things easier either as, mainly due to historical and political circumstances, the French, German and Russian languages were prioritized in Poland. The major source of information about Britain would then be school education (mainly history classes) and literature, including travel literature,[4] which would not make up for the lack of personal experience of the other.

One of the recurrent themes in veterans' recollections revolved around emotions. The imagined Britons were either devoid of emotions or successfully suppressing them. Consequently, they were believed to be reserved, cold and phlegmatic which, if approached from a negative perspective, could be taken for unfriendliness, inapproachability and snobbery. These British characteristics could be alien to Poles who were more prone to appeal to emotions. Edmund Lewandowski, in his book *Charakter narodowy Polaków i innych* [The National Character of Poles and Others] (2008), writes that both Poles and foreigners emphasised the role of emotions in the Polish national character. Among the attributes of Poles they mentioned: pursuit of strong impressions, inclination to exaggeration, and excitability. It was the heritage of the Middle Ages,

---

[4] To learn about the English and Celtic nations' literary relationships with Poland see Wojciech Lipoński, *Literatura polska XX wieku. Przewodnik Encyklopedyczny* [Polish literature of the 20th century. Encyclopaedic guide], Vol. 2 (Warszawa: Wydawnictwo Naukowe PWN), pp. 435—444 and 457—462.

Baroque, Romanticism and Roman Catholicism, rather than the Renaissance, Enlightenment and Positivism that distanced Poles from the typical British Protestant attributes, moderation being just one of them (Lewandowski 2008, 289). The differences led to both sides automatically attaching labels to each other. One of them would be the conviction about the "phlegmatic" disposition of the British nation. As seen through Polish visitors' eyes, the Western ally talked with phlegm (Pawłowicz 1991, 61), sailed ships "with their really proverbial phlegm" (Wroński 1981, 69) and their generals inspected bombed sites "with typical English phlegm" (Anders 1995, 227). These opinions invited comparisons to a tortoise. Trying to account for the British calm disposition, even in the context of war atrocities, the pilots asked rhetorically: "Is a tortoise afraid of a lion?" (Damsz 2009, 100). However, such statements could meet resistance from other colleagues who believed that their ally's strength was undervalued. Jerzy Damsz defended the Britons: "this phlegmatic 'British tortoise' more often reminded [us of] a lion which it has in its emblem anyway" (Ibid.). Another pilot, Bernard K. Buchwald (1999, 144), differentiated between the different nations of the British Isles, claiming that the Scots excelled in energy and temperament, but the Welsh made up for these characteristics with their directness, joy and love for singing and dancing. Only the English remained "terribly boring and phlegmatic" (Ibid.).

In accordance with the "typicality paradox"[5], what did not match the familiar picture was then considered an exception. A British captain whose vibrant personality did not fit the stereotype was said to have "the temperament and complexion of a southerner" (Nuszkiewicz 1983, 108). This description was aimed at putting distance between him and the "real" Briton. A similar effect was achieved by the introduction of the word "uncharacteristic". Thus a judo instructor who happened to be an energetic person was introduced as "a short, stocky fair-haired man with, uncharacteristically for an Englishman, a lively temperament" (Ibid., 97). British, or rather English phlegm, to stay true to Buchwald's observations, was opposed to perhaps more spontaneous, and hence more desirable, behaviour of Poles. Damsz recalled: "Bravado—any variety of it—was the order of the day with us. I can imagine that phlegmatic Englishmen many a time must have been surprised with many of our boys' devilish ideas"

---

[5] People having strong stereotypes tend to notice only those characteristics and behaviours of the stereotyped group members that confirm their preconceived notions. By implication, they consider group members displaying traits that stand in opposition to their stereotypical notions as untypical and thus unrepresentative which prevents any possibility of change of the stereotype, in: David. J. Schneider, *The Psychology of Stereotyping* (New York, London: Guilford Press 2005), p. 400.

(Ibid., 308). This bravado could be associated with another Polish trait, "ułańska fantazja" (literally "Lancer's fantasy"). It is a combination of bravery, imagination, creativity and emotionality of which many Poles were proud.

The concept of reserved Britons was not always taken for granted though. Examples of combatants admitting that a dissonance between widely held beliefs and reality did exist were common, even if they reflected superficial and/or temporary changes in perception. Those who discovered the discrepancies were irritated about misinformation and felt cheated:

> Actually, I should ask the authors of some pre-war books and novels about travelling through the British Isles a few questions. Where are these Britons, allegedly so unapproachable, so occupied with themselves and their matters? . . . where are these girls and women occupied with sport only, cold persons with hearts like chunks of ice, totally unable to show any emotions? (Sopoćko 2010, 29)

Disagreement with preconceptions could come in the form of critical remarks, but also in the form of elaborate insights into the problem, thus proving that veterans were active and keen observers of the reality, which many found new to them. Bohdan Wroński's collection of wartime reminiscences illustrates his commitment to bypassing mental shortcuts and working on the intricacies of intercultural communication. In the example that follows the reader will learn how Wroński's banal experience of being introduced as a new member of a British warship crew triggered an evolution of his reading of the Western ally. Used to traditional Polish hospitality and cordial relations, the sailor found the English procedure quite brusque, and his new colleagues' reaction unpleasantly indifferent:

> Enlistment was very simple. The deputy showed me my cabin and said: "You're at your home," and he was not interested in me anymore. I immediately became a crew member without any special favours or attention. Introducing me to officers was carried out in an equally ordinary, simple, English way. Several "How do you do's"—and this was it. Not even a shadow of interest in me. (1981, 65)

What Martha Gellhorn (1908—1998), an American writer and prominent war (including World War II) correspondent, could call "the [English] privacy of indifference" (in Paxman 1999, 129) and Jeremy Paxman could ascribe to "[English] natural reticence or a wish not to intrude" (Paxman 1999, 129), Wroński took for "'splendid isolation' towards a non-Briton" (Wroński 1981, 65). The passage of time, however, and the time spent with the British, encouraged reflection that actually his initial treatment on a warship was an expression of "higher hospitality" (Ibid.). It was an attempt to save him from any embarrassment that a new situation may have caused (Ibid.). Only a greater rooting in the British culture brought the sailor understanding of his hosts' love of privacy—"the dearest and most sacred part of an Englishman's nature"—which a newcomer would translate into nothing more than unsociability (Stowe, quoted in Langford 2000, 104). If the prerequisite of privacy is separateness, then "the ultimate form of separateness was the home itself" (Langford 2000, 104). By encouraging Wroński to feel at home on a ship, the English seaman offered the Pole "not a meeting-place, but, quite on the contrary, a place for personal privacy and seclusion" (Collier, quoted in Langford 2000, 104).

An equally valuable contribution to the cultural conditioning of emotions comes from Wiktor Tomaszewski. A doctor by profession and a soldier during the war, he was close to death. His stay in Scotland facilitated intercultural observations, including those related to the experience of death. "Among our fellow countrymen there is quite a widespread opinion about emotional insensitivity of the inhabitants of this island. For example, they are allegedly indifferent to their relatives' death. Is this true?"—he asked (Tomaszewski 1976, 115). Answering (negatively) to the question he came up with conclusions which sociologists and researchers of cultural studies would confirm—the intensity of pain we all suffer is similar, but we may differ in public manifestations of the suffering. This is a common phenomenon because, like other cultural expressions, emotions are culturally mediated. As Barker says: "Display rules regulate who can show what emotion to whom and to what degree under given circumstances" (2005, 143). Depending on the country, the characteristics of a neutral or affective culture[6] (to use Trompenaars' and Hampden-Turner's division) are displayed, though the degree to which it is done may also vary (Trompenaars and Hampden-Turner 1998, 69, 72—73). The Polish doctor captured the dichotomy by drawing the line between the outward and inward expression of grief: "Our Slavic race, similarly to the Latin one expresses its feelings on the

---

[6] Neutral cultures e.g. do not reveal what they are thinking or feeling (vs. affective ones display them verbally and non-verbally), emotions are often dammed up (vs. emotions flow easily, effusively) and cool and self-possessed conduct is admired (vs. heated, vital, animated expressions admired) in: Fons Trompenaars and Charles Hampden-Turner, *Riding the Waves of Culture. Understanding Cultural Diversity in Business* (London: Nicholas Brealey Publishing 1998), p. 79.

outside, often in a very demonstrative way. The British, on the other hand, display bigger discipline . . . Control of emotions belongs to good manners and is taught from childhood" (Tomaszewski 1976, 115).

Allies could learn the differences the hard way. Since emotions represent information which transfers meanings, the lack of knowledge about the meanings hampers communication (Trompenaars and Hampden-Turner 1998, 74). Tomaszewski reported a story told to him by a Polish army chaplain in which the British delegation attending the funeral of a Pole and totally unprepared for what was to come were shocked by their ally's grieving practises:

> The brother rushed at the deceased, started to pull him and take him out of the coffin, at the same time lamenting in an indescribable way. He had to be forcibly pulled away from the deceased and the coffin on which he lied down. The funeral participants, among them a group of Scots, were petrified at the terrible sight of this. (1976, 115)

Not always did the intensity and the display of emotions act to the Poles' disadvantage. This was the case with the expression of love and affection. After all, if death became commonplace during the war, so did love. This emotion inscribed itself into the "Live today, for tomorrow we die" motto, which put into words the search for deep positive feelings to counterbalance war miseries (Olson and Cloud 2004, 176). Slavic sojourners quickly became so popular with the local women that the native men started pretending to be Poles to attract the interest of the "fairer sex". Asked about the reason for this popularity, a Scotsman from Pruszyński's memoirs unpleasantly surprised his Polish listeners by attributing this attractiveness, at least in part, to lies spoken by the Slavs to females (Pruszyński 2010, 39). The provocative hypothesis relied, according to him, on the distinctiveness of traditions, which did not have a substantial influence on Poland. They pertained mainly to northern countries, which imposed a stricter moral code on the latter:

> Those cold northern countries are ruled by the severe law of the Scandinavian sagas and the stern code of the Old Testament, which ruthlessly punished the lies of Eve and of Cain, of Joseph's brothers and of Potiphar's unfaithful wife. . . . Things took quite a different turn with the Poles. The Scandinavian sagas reached the banks of the Vistula in a somewhat distorted and rather comic way; as for instance, the story about the king who was eaten by mice. Catholicism replaced the gloomy accounts of the misdeeds of the early Hebrews with colourful and human stories about the lives of the saints. (Ibid., 39—40)

The soft nature of Slavs, sensitive to the works of Roman and Italian poets (Ovid, Petrarch) from whom they had learnt how to speak of love beautifully, but not necessarily with truth, together with the advantage of being more expressive and exotic, made them more appealing to British women, whose expectations of a perfect relationship had been additionally shaped by the romantic images promoted by the Hollywood film industry (Ibid., 40—45). Similarly to Tomaszewski, the Scot denied the claim that the British (here British men) are, to borrow the expression from Trompenaars and Hampden-Turner, "emotionally dead", but underlined their culturally different manifestation and sublimation of feelings into "undertones, whispers, delicate hints" (Trompenaars and Hampden-Turner 1998, 41).

From an intercultural point of view, this Scotsman's opinion can be particularly valuable, not only because it shows the British perspective on the passionate Poles/dispassionate Britons issue, but because it can be taken as an example of how stereotypes come into existence. Each fact in itself, delivered by the Scottish narrator, can be accepted as historically and culturally proven true—after all, there *are* Scandinavian sagas, there *are* Greek philosophers he mentions and there *is* this kind of Puritanism which instilled fear in people (for example John Knox was progressive in the sense of education, but he was very dogmatic in the sense of religion). What is more, researchers do distinguish between universalist (rule based) and particularist (relation based more than rule based) societies, in which Protestants tend to belong more often to the first group and Catholics to the other (Trompenaars and Hampden-Turner 1998, 35—36). However, the end product of the Scotsman's presentation, the proof why the Poles are found so attractive by the opposite sex, is unconvincing. Sold in a very intelligent way by an educated and erudite person, the hypothesis remains a very personal and subjective opinion.

"War is a great teacher of geography, helping to make discoveries hardly less startling than those of Columbus or of Cook", noted Ksawery Pruszyński (2010, 6) in the first chapter of his war accounts, reminding his readers of the easily forgotten and/or belittled aspect of war—the war perceived as a travel and servicemen as observers of human cultures and interactions. Polish combatants' journey north confirmed this. The migration enforced by the military developments of 1939 and 1940, which aimed to achieve the continuation of an armed struggle to obtain political gains, which would ultimately make re-establishing a free country possible, proved that Poles were more than fighting automatons and the war was more than a battleground. The position of a cultural outsider, which each serviceman found themselves in when arriving to the British

Isles in their capacity as a Polish ally, was incomparable to their status of soldiers, but it could also pose a great challenge. Unable to dispose of the cultural baggage they brought with them, they struggled to make sense of the unknown world around them in much more demanding circumstances than a peacetime visitor would do. The north they observed as tourists triggered layers of patriotism, just as the combat they were in did. Adverse weather conditions reminded them of more friendly landscapes they had left behind, and provoked homesickness and melancholic feelings. Away from the frontline, encounters with the British other reinforced the stereotypes about the "cold-natured" nation. For some, this became an identity exercise because, by comparing cultures, they learnt more about their individual and national identities. For others this was an exercise in deconstruction, as they were ready to form their own judgements and abandon stereotypical notions. In both cases, it was a hard mental labour.

The question that might be asked is if this "discovery aspect" was a worthwhile part of their wartime existence. The answer is positive. Wartime tourism can be considered a cognitive bonus, but it should be reiterated that one cannot underestimate its motivational and protective function which substantially contributed to these combatants' psychological wellbeing, and thus indirectly also to their physical survival:

> It is possible that one of the ways of coping with the horror [of war] . . . was this tourist stance which . . . always implied they were observers, not participants, and maintained a protective barrier between the observer and the observed. The tourist is uninvolved, and this precious detachment, the capacity to stand aside for a time, might have been a crucial respite in war. (White 1997, 126)

References

Anders, Władysław. 1995. *Bez ostatniego rozdziału. Wspomnienia z lat 1939—1945*. Lublin: Wydawnictwo.

Barker, Chris. 2005. *Cultural Studies. Theory and Practice*. London, Thousand Oaks, New Delhi: SAGE Publications.

Buchwald, Bernard Karol. 1999. *Od Wrony do Spitfire'a. Wspomnienia pilota*. Poznań: „Comp-Druk".

Burton, Robert. 2004, accessed September 18, 2016, http://www.gutenberg.org/files/10800/10800-h/10800-h.htm

Cambridge Dictionary. True North, accessed September 24, 2016, http://dictionary.cambridge.org/dictionary/english/true-north

Collier, Price. 1909. *England and the English from an American Point of View*. London: C. Scribner's Sons.

Cox, John D. 2005. *Travelling South. Travel Narratives and the Construction of American Identity*. Athens and London: The University of Georgia Press.

Cunningham, Valentine. 1988. *British Writers of the Thirties*. Oxford, New York: Oxford University Press.

Daly, Gavin. 2013. *The British Soldier in the Peninsular War. Encounters with Spain and Portugal, 1808—1814*. Houndmills: Palgrave Macmillan.

Damsz, Jerzy. 2009. *Lwowskie Puchacze. Wspomnienia lotnika*. Kraków: Wydawnictwo Znak.

Davidson, Peter. 2005. *The Idea of North*. London: Reaktion Books.

Fussell, Paul, ed. 1987. *The Norton Book of Travel*. New York: W. W. Norton.

Hulan, Renée. 2002. *Northern Experience and the Myths of Canadian Cultur*. Montreal & Kingston, London, Ithaca: McGill-Queen's University Press.

Jasiakiewicz, Wojciech. 2010. *"Woefullest Of Nations" or "European America"? British Travel Accounts of Poland 1863*. Bydgosz: Wydawnictwo Uniwersytetu Kazimierza Wielkiego.

Langford, Paul. 2000. *Englishness Identified. Manners and Character 1650—1850*. Oxford: Oxford University Press.

Leighton, James S. 2013. *Witnessing the Revolutionary and Napoleonic Wars in German Central Europe*. Basingstoke: Palgrave Macmillan.

Lewandowski, Edmund. 2008. *Charakter narodowy Polaków i innych*. Warszawa: MUZA SA.

Łaszkiewicz, Stefan. 1982. *Od Cambrai po Coventry*. Warszawa: Ministerstwo Obrony Narodowej.

MacCannell, Dean. 1999. *The Tourist. A New Theory of the Leisure Class*. Berkeley, Los Angeles, London: University of California Press.

McNaylor, Mitchell. 2003. "Military Memoirs". In *Literature of Travel and Exploration. An Encyclopedia*, edited by Jennifer Speake, 795—6. London and New York: Routledge.

Microsoft (R) Encarta (R) 97 Encyclopaedia. (c.) 1993—1996. Microsoft Corporation.

Nuszkiewicz, Ryszard. 1983. *Uparci*. Warszawa: Instytut Wydawniczy Pax.

Olson, Lynne, and Stanley Cloud. 2004. *A Question of Honour. The Kosciuszko Squadron: Forgotten Heroes of World War II*. New York: Vintage Books.

Pawłowicz, Bohdan. 1991. *Krew na oceanie*. Warszawa: Oficyna Wydawnicza.

Paxman, Jeremy. 1999. *The English. A Portrait of a People*. London: Penguin Books.

Poland and Poles in the Second World War, accessed September 25, 2016, https://ww2.pl/polish-armed-forces-in-the-west/

Pruszyński, Ksawery. 2010. *Polish Invasion*. Edinburgh: Birlinn.

Schneider, David. J. 2005. *The Psychology of Stereotyping*. New York, London: Guilford Press.

Smethurst, Paul. 2003. "Tourism". In *Literature of Travel and Exploration. An Encyclopedia*, edited by Jennifer Speake, 1185—7. London and New York: Routledge.

Sopoćko, Eryk. 2010. Patrole "Orła". Gdańsk: Finna.

Speake, Jennifer. 2003. "Preface". In *Literature of Travel and Exploration. An Encyclopedia*, edited by Jennifer Speake, vii—viii. London and New York: Routledge.

Struk, Janina. 2011. *Private Pictures. Soldiers Inside View of War*. London, New York: I.B. Tauris.

Tomaszewski, Wiktor. 1976. *Na szkockiej ziemi. Wspomnienia wojenne ze służby zdrowia i z Polskiego Wydziału Lekarskiego w Edynburgu*. Londyn: The White Eagle Press.

Trompenaars, Fons, and Charles Hampden-Turner. 1998. *Riding the Waves of Culture. Understanding Cultural Diversity in Business*. London: Nicholas Brealey Publishing.

White, Richard. 1997. "The Soldier as Tourist: The Australian Experience of the Great War". *Kunapipi*, Vol: 18, No. 2, 3, 117—29.

Wasilewski, Antoni. 1978. *W szkocką kratę*. Kraków: Wydawnictwo Literackie.

Wroński, Bohdan. 1981. *Wspomnienia płyną jak okręty*. Londyn: Odnowa.

Zapisane w Kronikach, accessed September 25, 2016, http://www.zapisanewkronikach.pl/2014/01/turysci-sikorskiego.html

Żegota-Januszajtis, Jerzy Zbigniew. 2006. *Wspomnienia fotoreportera z Dywizji Maczka*. Kraków: Towarzystwo Słowaków w Polsce.

CHAPTER SEVEN

MOVING SOUTH TO ENVISION THE NORTH: SEAMUS HEANEY'S *NORTH*

KAREN PATRICK KNUTSEN

The Poet in Exile

This paper concerns a particular transitional stage in the Nobel Prize-winning poetry of Irish writer Seamus Heaney (1939—2013)—as expressed in the collection *North* (1975). During the Troubles of the late 1960s and early 1970s in Northern Ireland, Heaney, an Irish Catholic and prominent intellectual, was under public pressure to take a political stance in his writing by either supporting or condemning the republican cause. He refused, insisting that poetry should not be forced to play a part in political struggles. Consequently, he left his post at Queen's University in Belfast in 1972, and moved south to become a citizen of the Irish Republic. *North* was the first volume of poetry he published after his move.

Summing up *North*, the critic Henry Hart writes: "Heaney wrestles with the call to become more politically engaged and ultimately resists it for the safer, more private ardours of poetry" (1992, 76).[1] Although Hart's judgement is partially true, I argue here that in *North* Heaney is reorienting himself after his move, and this involves remapping his understanding of

---

[1] *North* had a quite mixed reception, with British and Irish commentators diverging in their emphases. A number of British critics responded to and praised the style and content of the collection. However, as Edna Longley points out (1994, 66), the Irish critic "[Conor Cruise] O'Brien's informed response established a native line of comment on *North*, including contributions by its author, that raises the most fundamental questions about the relationship between literature and politics." Whereas O'Brien felt that reading the poems gave an uncanny feeling of understanding the historical agony of the Catholics in Northern Ireland, Longley herself and a number of other critics objected to Heaney's use of idiom, especially in part one of the collection, which "often falls between the stools of poetry and politics instead of building a mythic bridge" (Ibid., 74).

both history and poetry. His displacement meant that he had to expand his own sense of place, and to develop a new identity as a writer. To do so he needed to imagine a home space that had been traversed and affected by different peoples, interests and histories (Malone 2000, 1103). He revises his poetic "manifesto", creating a new "country of the mind", which expands to encompass the geography and cultures of northern Europe rather than simply his native Ulster. Moreover, *North* set the premises for Heaney's later poetry, outlining issues he continued to address: a sense of place and belonging, and his problematic, hybrid heritage, both politically and in terms of language. In the following I trace these developments in readings of selected poems from the collection.

Digging into History

Many poets have spoken of the ways they envision their art, usually through poetic tropes. Dylan Thomas's poetry, for example, conveys the idea that the mission of the poet is to enchant, to cast a spell on the listeners by overwhelming them with musical language.[2] In contrast, W. H. Auden believed that poetry should lead to meditation and reflection, rather than enchantment and enthusiasm. Many of Auden's early poems thematize the concerns of the left-wing political activist. Later poems could be raucous and celebratory, but most of his mature work is contemplative, focused on philosophical inquiry and spirituality (Izzo 2004, 3—5). A third writer, former British poet laureate Ted Hughes described poetry as "capturing animals" and he often used the predator motif in his poems. He compared writing poetry to hunting and believed that a poem is a new species of creature, a new species of life outside our own (1961, 15—31).

So how did Heaney envision his crafting of poetry? The poem "Digging" published in *Death of a Naturalist* (1966, 1—2) has often been read as Heaney's poetic "manifesto" or "ars poetica"—a poem about the process or idea of writing poetry. Sitting down to write, the speaker notes:

---

[2] As John Ackerman explains, "meaning in a poem by Thomas is compounded as much in the emotional and sensory impact as in the intellectual or conceptual import. Indeed, the ideas that inform Thomas's early, as his later verse, are few and relatively simple; what is original and striking is their enactment in image and sound structure. The world the poem creates is physically exciting, sonorous and hypnotic in effect, intuitional as well as emotive and sensory in its communication" (1994, 75). As the many manuscript versions of his poems indicate, Thomas worked hard to create the musical, incantatory effect of his individual poems.

"Between my finger and my thumb / The squat pen rests; snug as a gun." The comparison of pen and gun brings to mind the adage that "The pen is mightier than the sword", and suggests that poetry can function as a political force, although a non-violent one. The speaker ends the poem by repeating: "Between my finger and my thumb / The squat pen rests. / I'll dig with it." He chooses the pen, rather than the spade of his forefathers or the gun of Northern Irish sectarian violence as his vocational "tool". Digging becomes his metaphor for creating poetry: digging into the soil of his native ground, into the historic past and into the living roots of his own head.

The speaker builds up this conceit of digging by conjuring up images of his ancestors: "My grandfather cut more turf in a day / Than any other man on Toner's bog." He sees his father who "Bends low, comes up twenty years away / Stooping in rhythm through potato drills / where he was digging." The emblematic potato, so important in Irish history that potato blight (1845—1849) led to the death and emigration of millions is woven into the speaker's childhood memories; his father roots out the plants "To scatter new potatoes that we picked / Loving their cool hardness in our hands." In spite of these memories and his ancestral rootedness in Irish soil, the speaker concludes: "But I've no spade to follow men like them." Instead he sees writing poetry as his true vocation and as a means of coping with the historical and contemporary injustices of a divided Ireland.

Writing about his own work and that of other writers, Heaney demonstrated a long-term preoccupation with the unstable role of place in the creative process, as Ronald Schuchard points out in the introduction to Heaney's essays in *The Place of Writing*:

> The aura of place imposes itself on one poet's imagination; another poet imposes his singular vision on a plural place; places become havens or heavens; they drive the poet into spiritual or physical exile; they provide poetry with its nourishment and its distraction; they liberate imagination and darkened consciousness. (1989, 4)

Heaney was concerned with the voices of Irish writers in general and argued that poets like William Butler Yeats, Patrick Kavanagh and John Montague poetically engaged their respective geographical places in order to create a "country of the mind". Seeing the poet as rooted in his historical place in a particular geographical location generates, as Schuchard puts it, "a dialogue between the aims of art and the claims of history, between an emerging artistic consciousness and a persistent historical conscience" (Ibid.). For Heaney, poetry needed to maintain a relationship with place in order to come to terms with the past.

In part one of *North,* Heaney begins with a poem that, like "Digging", was written in 1966. The poem is entitled "Antaeus", and serves to ground the collection. The poet-speaker envisions himself as the mythological Greek giant Antaeus, who challenged all passers-by to fight with him, well-knowing, that as long as he kept physically in touch with the earth beneath him he could not be conquered. "When I lie on the ground / I rise flushed as a rose in the morning. / In fights I arrange a fall on the ring / To rub myself with sand / That is operative / As an elixir. I cannot be weaned / Off the earth's long contour, her river-veins. / Down here in my cave," (1975, 3). Here Heaney establishes a sense of place, the rootedness that shaped his identity as a poet, his sense of belonging and purpose that was so much a part of his original ars poetica. But the poem ends with a foreshadowing: "Among sky-born and royal: / He may well throw me and renew my birth / But let him not plan, lifting me off the earth, / My elevation, my fall." And part one of *North* ends with the poem "Hercules and Antaeus", written in 1975, where disaster strikes. Hercules the hero, as one of his seven tasks, fights Antaeus: "Hercules lifts his arms / in a remorseless V, / his triumph unassailed / by the powers he has shaken, / and lifts and banks Antaeus / high as a profiled ridge, /a sleeping giant, / pap for the dispossessed" (1975, 46—47). The hero Antaeus, separated from what gives him power, the earth, is a fallen giant, a repudiated myth. The poet-speaker, like Antaeus has lost contact with his home ground and can no longer speak with authority as a poet: His words have been reduced to "pap", something lacking solid value or sustenance, suitable only for the dispossessed. Heaney has lost his "sense of place" and laments this loss. These two poems frame 16 other poems which explore the history of Ireland and the history of northern Europe, superimposing culture upon culture and delineating invasion after invasion.

In Western culture, north is specifically treated as *the* fundamental or cardinal direction, reflecting quite arbitrary historical factors. And of course what is "north" is relative to your own position. Just think how strange it seems to study an inverted world map from our Westernized perspective, where the other directions on the compass are relative and we navigate following the North Star. Moving south in a sense turned Heaney's world upside down. Uprooted and relocated in County Wicklow and later in Dublin, he continued to look north, and north becomes *the* cardinal direction used to map and define Irish culture and history in his first poetry collection published after his move. Here the concept of the north forms a mythical touchstone for exploring the people, history and landscape of all of Ireland, refracted through images of Northern European experience, especially the Scandinavian and English invasions. As Christopher T. Malone argues, discussing the poetry of both Heaney and Paul Muldoon, "To re-imagine the world and its spatial coordinates, without preconceived order or direction, to seek out an impossible past, with hope and without it, allows a new sense of national community to emerge" (2000, 1105). The poems give us a survey of the development of "a myth that allowed [Heaney] to articulate a vision of Ireland—its people, history and landscape" as the blurb on the book so succinctly puts it. In my reading however, Heaney builds up this myth, only to dismiss it. He understands that myth-building is dangerous; it can sustain violence by idealizing death and immortalizing mundane humans who kill for petty, personal reasons.

North is divided into two distinct parts.[3] Part one is where Heaney envisions the mythic aspects of the north. Part two turns to the Troubles of the 1960s and 70s and presents a self-portrait of the poet in exile. In this way, *North* documents the poet's process of mapping a new, hybrid space. He is attempting to find his position in the world, in poetry, in Ireland, within the Troubles, and lastly, but perhaps most importantly, within language. Tellingly, manuscript versions of the poem "North", which gives the collection its title, reveal that it changed from "North Atlantic" to "Northerners" to simply "North" as he worked his way through.[4] The idea of the north and a northern identity grew larger and larger, away from a specific location or population. It became mythic rather than concrete, and was rejected, in favor of a deeper understanding of history and human nature.

In "Belderg", for example, the speaker visits an excavated, Neolithic settlement in County Mayo, Ireland dating to 3000 B.C. Here great quernstones have worked their way out of the soil, and the excavation reveals the marks of prehistoric cultures: "There were first plough-marks, / The stone-age fields, the tomb / Corbelled, turfed and chambered, / Floored with dry turf-coomb" (1975, 4). The stone-wall patternings of the past are "Repeated before our eyes / In the stone walls of Mayo" (Ibid.). The speaker has a conversation with a person he meets at Belderg, and they reflect on these layers. The poet mentions the name of his family's farm in County Derry, Mossbawn, and they reflect on the etymology of the name—its possible Irish, Norse, and English roots. The speaker

---

[3] See David Lloyd's article "The Two Voices of Seamus Heaney's *North*" (1979, 5—13) for an enlightening discussion of this two part structure.

[4] See "The Manuscript Drafts of the poem '**North**'" in Curtis, Tony (ed.), *The Art of Seamus Heaney*. Mid Glamorgan, Wales: Seren Books, 1994 [1992], 53—61.

reflects on how all of these civilizations have become so mixed, so inseparable—they are like "Grist to an ancient mill, / And in my mind's eye [I] saw / A world-tree of balanced stones, / Querns piled like vertebrae, / The marrow crushed to grounds" (Ibid., 5). Connections are made here between artefacts, peoples, myths, cultures and ancient languages, and they are all an integral part of the speaker's identity. One can no longer separate an Irish, a Norse, or an English strain here. The superimposition of culture upon culture throughout history leads the speaker to recognize the hybridity of all cultures and identities.

Heaney's "digging" takes him clear back to the Iron Age in the so-called "bog poems" in *North* where he reflects on the preserved bodies intermittently dug up in the bogs of Northern Europe. Some of these bodies were later studied, speculated upon, and put on display in Danish museums and museums in other countries. The topic of the "Going North" conference is not simply the concept of north, but also aspects of travel and intercultural communication. And Heaney, did in fact travel farther north, to Denmark at one point to see some of these bog bodies and to meet the Danish archaeologist P. V. Glob, who speculated on who these people had been, and why they were murdered and hidden in the boggy ground that preserved them, skin blackened, yet intact, swathes of hair and clothing left behind; even the stomach contents of some victims were analyzed, revealing the make-up of their last meals (Glob 1969). Glob's theories on the bodies as sacrificial victims to the earth goddess, planted in the bog to ensure the return of warm weather and growing conditions for food needed by the clan, or as victims of ritual punishment fired Heaney's imagination.

The poems inspired by this experience draw lines between the brutal past and the contemporary violence of the Troubles. Heaney, like a number of other Irish poets, envisioned Ireland as Cathleen Ní Houlihan, a female personification of Ireland, often used as a mythical symbol and emblem of Irish nationalism in literature and art.[5] Originally an old woman thrown off her farm and land, she relentlessly demands blood sacrifice from her children, and when young men die for her she is rejuvenated. Heaney sees her as a parallel to the earth goddess of Glob's Iron Age, and views his violent countrymen as willingly, cyclically, and meaninglessly acquiescing to the blood sacrifice. His guilt about leaving his native Ulster, and his continual digging into the past led to poems of great anguish and beauty which led him to another physical journey to the north,

---

[5] See for example W. B. Yeats' and Lady Gregory's play *Cathleen Ní Houlihan* (c. 1912) for an example of how the emblem is used.

in 1995, when he travelled to Stockholm to collect the Nobel Prize in literature. It was awarded by the committee "for works of lyrical beauty and ethical depth, which exalt everyday miracles and the living past" ("The Nobel Prize in Literature 1995", 2016).

Ireland was England's first colony, invaded by Anglo-Norman troops as early as 1169. The native Celts were colonized, and a new language was gradually imposed upon them. Like other post-colonial writers, Heaney has an uneasy attitude to the colonial language English. Some of the key preoccupations of post-colonial studies are expressed in Heaney's poems: nation, language, place, race and identity. In the next poem, these preoccupations persist.

In the poem "North", facing the North Atlantic and looking toward Iceland and Greenland, the speaker reflects on the Viking heritage of Ireland. He describes these mythological invaders as "those fabulous raiders, those lying in Orkney and Dublin / measured against their long swords rusting, / those in the solid belly of stone ships, / those hacked and glinting / in the gravel of thawed streams / were ocean-deafened voices / warning me, lifted again / in violence and epiphany" (1975, 10). Images of Thor's hammer, Viking ships and brutal battle are juxtaposed with "geography and trade, / thick-witted couplings and revenges, / the hatreds and behindbacks / of the althing, lies and women, / exhaustions nominated peace, / memory incubating the spilled blood" (Ibid., 10—11). The mythological Norsemen are reduced to vindictive, self-centered trouble-makers, and their blood feuds are reprehensible, bloodshed leading to more bloodshed. One cannot help but associate with the revenge killings and punishments going on in Ulster at the time that *North* was published, indirectly suggesting a condemnation of both sides in the sectarian violence. The speaker rejects these Viking heroes and vows to focus on a different type of legacy: The tongue of the dragon-headed Viking ship commands him to "Lie down / in the word-hoard, burrow / the coil and gleam / of your furrowed brain. / Compose in darkness. / Expect aurora borealis / in the long foray / but no cascade of light." (Ibid., 11). Language and poetry will continue to be his treasure and vocation, the foundation of his hybrid identity and source of inspiration. It is perhaps these lines that led to Hart's contention that Heaney had left political topics behind in order to focus on the "more private ardours of poetry" (1992, 76), yet the theme of brutal colonialization is highly evident in the poem as well.

In a series of poems in the middle of part one Heaney contemplates a number of the bog bodies found in Northern Europe, again literally digging to reveal and understand the past. Two of the bodies are identifiable—the male in "The Grauballe Man" was found in Denmark and the "little adultress", the Windeby girl, was found in Northern Germany, and later determined to be a young boy rather than a girl. In both poems Heaney poetically describes the bodies, amazed over how human and recognizable as individuals they remain after so many centuries in the bog. Of the Grauballe Man he asks: "Who will say 'corpse' / to his vivid cast? / Who will say 'body' / to his opaque repose?" (Heaney 1975, 29). He finds the victim "hung in the scales / with beauty and atrocity;" (Ibid.); both fascinating in his peaceful repose and horrifying because the viewer understands, seeing the corpse's slit throat, the bestiality of his murder. The final stanza carries us forward in time, where Heaney juxtaposes this victim to contemporary victims of sectarian violence in Ulster, to "the actual weight / of each hooded victim, / slashed and dumped" (Ibid.). Heaney admitted that it was in fact easier to view and think about these Iron Age victims than about contemporary victims in his own native country:

> My emotions, my feelings, whatever those instinctive energies are that have to be engaged for a poem, those energies quickened more when contemplating a victim, strangely, from 2,000 years ago than they did from contemplating a man at the end of a road being swept up into a plastic bag—I mean the barman at the end of our road tried to carry out a bomb and it blew up. Now there is of course something terrible about that, but somehow language, words didn't live in the way I think they have to live in a poem when they were hovering over that kind of horror and pity. (Heaney 1997)

Similarly, in "Punishment" the speaker begins by describing the dead girl and identifying himself with her. Later he steps back and labels himself an "artful voyeur", and finally he imagines himself as one of the people in the crowd that condemned her to death and executed her: "I almost love you / but would have cast, I know / the stones of silence" (Heaney 1975, 31). Here he again draws parallels to the punishments carried out in Ulster. Irish girls who consorted with British soldiers were often stripped naked, their hair shaven from their heads, cauled in tar and chained to railings to be shamed in public. The speaker has not spoken up against this treatment and admits that he "would connive / in civilized outrage / yet understand the exact / and tribal, intimate revenge" (Ibid.). Despite all our advances in civilization, the tribal instincts remain.

Finally, I would like to turn to the last poem in *North,* number 6, entitled "Exposure" (Ibid., 67—68). Set in Wicklow in December, the poet wanders through a winter landscape feeling depressed and disentitled: "How did I end up like this? / I often think of my friends' / Beautiful prismatic counselling / And the anvil brains of some who hate me / As I sit weighing and weighing / My responsible *tristia.* / For what? For the ear? For the people? / For what is said behind-backs?" (Ibid., 67). In spite of his negotiations of identity in the foregoing poems, he cannot help but feel left out during a portentous time in the history of his native country. He also feels guilt at having abandoned Ulster, now living as an exile: "I am neither internee nor informer; An inner émigré, grown long-haired / And thoughtful; a wood-kerne / Escaped from the massacre, / Taking protective colouring / From bole and bark, feeling / Every wind that blows; / Who, blowing up these sparks / For their meagre heat, have missed / The once-in-a-lifetime portent, / The comet's pulsing rose" (Ibid., 68).

North as a "Country of the Mind"

As I initially pointed out, I view *North* as a pivotal stepping stone documenting Heaney's redefinition of his identity and his sense of place in the world. The concept of north gradually expands in this volume to encompass Northern Europe, with its multiple cultures, superimposed one upon another in Ireland. But *North* also says a lot about the *place*—or purpose—of Heaney's writing in that world; it delineates how history continues to impact our daily lives both personally and politically; how poetry can lead to a deeper understanding of the past; and finally, *North* challenges readers to break out of meaningless cycles of violence and atrocity.

References

Ackerman, John. 1994 [1991]. *A Dylan Thomas Companion.* London: Macmillan.

Curtis, Tony. ed. 1994 [1992]. *The Art of Seamus Heaney.* Mid Glamorgan, Wales: Seren Books.

Izzo, David Garrett. 2004. *W. H. Auden Encyclopedia.* Jefferson, NC and London: McFarlane & Co. Inc., Publishers.

Glob, P. V. 1969 [1965]. *The Bog People: Iron-Age Man Preserved.* Translated by Rupert Bruce-Mitford. London: Faber and Faber.

Hart, Henry. 1992. *Seamus Heaney: Poet of Contrary Progressions.* New York: Syracuse University Press.

Heaney, Seamus. 1966. *Death of a Naturalist.* London and Boston: Faber and Faber.

—. 1975. *North.* London: Faber and Faber.

—. 1984 [1980]. "The Sense of Place" in *Preoccupations: Selected Prose 1968—1978.* London and Boston: Faber and Faber, 13—49.

—. 1989. *The Place of Writing*. Atlanta, GA: Scholars Press.

—. 1994 [1992]. "The Manuscript Drafts of the poem 'North'". In *The Art of Seamus Heaney*, edited by Tony Curtis, 53—62. Mid Glamorgan, Wales: Seren Books,.

—. 1995. *The Redress of Poetry*. London: Faber and Faber.

—. 1997. Interview with Brian Donnelly. Copenhagen: Danmarks Radio.

Hughes, Ted. 2008 [1967]. "Capturing Animals". In Ted Hughes, *Poetry in the Making: A handbook for writing and teaching*. London: Faber and Faber, 15—31.

Longley, Edna. 1994 [1992]. "*North*: 'Inner Emigré' or 'Artful Voyeur'?" *The Art of Seamus Heaney*, edited by Tony Curtis, 63—96. Mid Glamorgan, Wales: Seren Books,.

Malone, Christopher T. 2000. "Writing Home: Spatial Allegories in the Poetry of Seamus Heaney and Paul Muldoon". *ELH*, Vol: 67, No. 4, 1083—1109.

Schuchard, Ronald. 1989. "Introduction". In Seamus Heaney, *The Place of Writing*. Atlanta, GA: Scholars Press, 2—16.

"The Nobel Prize in Literature 1995". 2014. *Nobelprize.org*. Nobel Media AB, accessed February 10, 2016, http://www.nobelprize.org/nobel_prizes/literature/laureates/1995/

Further Reading

Bolton, Jonathan. 2001. "'Customary Rhythms': Seamus Heaney and the Rite of Poetry". In *Papers on Language and Literature,* Vol: 37, No. 2, (Spring), 205—22.

Corcoran, Neil. 1998. "Extracts from 'Writing a Bare Wire: Station Island (1984)'" in *The Poetry of Seamus Heaney: A Critical Study*. London: Faber and Faber, 110—11; 114—25". Reprinted in *Twentieth-Century British and Irish Poetry: Hardy to Mahon*, 2011, edited by Michael O'Neill and Madeleine Callaghan. Oxford: Blackwell-Wiley, 250—9.

Culingford, Elizabeth Butler. 1996. "British Romans and Irish Cathaginians: Anticolonial Metaphor in Heaney, Friel, and McGuinness". *PMLA*, Vol: 111, No. 2 (March), 222—39.

Garret, Yvonne C. 2011. "'King of Infinite Space': Structures of Hybridity in the Poetry of Seamus Heaney". Irish-GA 1421 Debates in Modern Irish History, December 18, accessed January 8, 2015, https://www.academia.edu/7950293/_King_of_Infinite_Space_Structur es_of_Hybridity_in_the_Poetry_of_Seamus_Heaney

Lloyd, David. 1979. "The Two Voices of Seamus Heaney's *North*". *Ariel: A Review of International English Literature,* Vol: 10, Issue 4, 5—13.

Mollerin, Kaja Schjerven. 2012. "Å høre til" [A sense of belonging, my trans.] Bokmagasinet, *Klassekampen,* Sat. 7. Sept., 12—3.

O'Neill, Michael & Madeleine Callaghan, eds. 2011. "Northern Irish Poetry: The Poles of Our Condition—Seamus Heaney and Derek Mahon". In *Twentieth-Century British and Irish Poetry: Hardy to Mahon.* Oxford: Blackwell-Wiley, 245—66.

Purdy, Anthony. 2002. "The Bog Body as Mnemotope: Nationalist Archaeologies in Heaney and Tournier". *Style,* Vol: 36, No. 1, Spring, 93—110.

proposed economic utopia would put an end to slavery, but would perpetuate the white possession of Africa in a new kind of servitude.

In *The Interesting Narrative*, Equiano reports on his northward journey "nearly as far towards the Pole as 81 degrees north, and 20 degrees east longitude", which, according to him, is farther than anyone had traveled at the time. The description of the Arctic expedition occupies the latter part of Chapter IX, whose title reads: "The author arrives at Martinico—Meets with new difficulties—Gets to Montserrat, where he takes leave of his old master, and sails for England—Meets Capt. Pascal—Learns the French horn—Hires himself with Doctor Irving, where he learns to freshen sea water—Leaves the doctor, and goes a voyage to Turkey and Portugal; and afterwards goes a voyage to Grenada, and another to Jamaica—Returns to the Doctor, and they embark together on a voyage to the North Pole, with the Hon. Capt. Phipps—Some account of that voyage, and the dangers the author was in—He returns to England" (Equiano 2005, n.p.). The title may reveal the denouement, but does promise a thrilling story. Indeed, Equiano's otherwise fastidious account gains dramatic overtones as the crew approach the North Pole.

The Arctic trip is only one part of Equiano's extensive sea journeys, but it is the last adventure before his return to England and conversion to Christianity. The protagonist embarks on such faraway journeys not only for material gain or a sense of destination and purpose, but also for admittedly "being still of a roving disposition, and desirous of seeing as many different parts of the world as I could" (Equiano 2005, n.p.); he then declares himself "tired of the sea" and returns in the service of his master on land, but not before long is "roused by the sound of fame"; this last time, the call is "to seek new adventures, and to find, towards the north pole, what our Creator never intended we should, a passage to India" (Equiano 2005, n.p.). Thus, on the 24th day of May 1773, Equiano joins his master on an expedition to explore a north-east passage, conducted by John Constantine Phipps, on board the Race Horse.

Equiano's factual reporting of time, place and daily events makes for a trustworthy account of an actual journey to the North Pole. This is, nevertheless, a very personal tale, which contains the traveler's own perspective and experiences. The travel writer is so truthful that he admits to negligently starting a fire on the ship; nevertheless, the account focuses on his individual circumstances and danger rather than on the greater perils involved. As the protagonist "had resolved to keep a journal of this singular and interesting voyage", he goes about writing it in the doctor's store-room, which is stuffed with combustibles. The inevitable occurs: "Unfortunately it happened in the evening as I was writing my journal, that I had occasion to take the candle out of the lanthorn, and a spark having touched a single thread of the tow, all the rest caught the flame, and immediately the whole was in a blaze" (Equiano 2005, n.p.). At this point the narrative turns inward, as Equiano dwells on his own reactions and thoughts at the time of the accident: "I saw nothing but present death before me, and expected to be the first to perish in the flames", but does note that, after being saved by fellow crewmen, he was "severely reprimanded and menaced" (Equiano 2005, n.p.). Nevertheless, he takes the liberty to mention that "even my own fears made me give heed to this command for a little time" and resumes the writing of his journal; this is proof of the protagonist having a mind of his own, but also a leitmotif confirming once again the crucial importance of authorship in the African-American tradition.

As the ship sails to the North Pole, the landscape and the day-night cycle change: "On the 28th of June, being in lat. 78, we made Greenland, where I was surprised to see the sun did not set" (Equiano 2005, n.p.). The protagonist notates diligently the visible differences in weather, relief and fauna: "The weather now became extremely cold; and as we sailed between north and east, which was our course, we saw many very high and curious mountains of ice; and also a great number of very large whales, which used to come close to our ship, and blow the water up to a very great height in the air" (Equiano 2005, n.p.).

But the northbound expedition soon reaches a halt: "On the 29th and 30th of July we saw one continued plain of smooth unbroken ice, bounded only by the horizon; and we fastened to a piece of ice that was eight yards eleven inches thick" (Equiano 2005, n.p.). The account now focuses on ship activities; the crew is busy hunting and fishing for survival: "We killed many different animals at this time, and among the rest nine bears" (Equiano 2005, n.p.). Not all local encounters are lucky and Equiano reports one such incident, with detachment: "Some of our people once, in the boat, fired at and wounded a sea-horse, which dived immediately; and, in a little time after, brought up with it a number of others. They all joined in an attack upon the boat, and were with difficulty prevented from staving or oversetting her" (Equiano 2005, n.p.).

The crew seems to become settled in the unfriendly environment, but the situation escalates shortly: "We remained hereabouts until the 1st of August; when the two ships got completely fastened in the ice, occasioned by the loose ice that set in from the sea" (Equiano 2005, n.p.). This is no longer a personal accident but a threat to everyone's survival and the protagonist will, from this point onwards, identify with the crew and use the first person plural: "This made our situation very dreadful and

Du Bois, W. E. B. 1903. *The Souls of Black Folk*. New York: Dover Publications.

Equiano, Olaudah. 1789. *The Interesting Narrative of the Life of 'Olaudah Equiano' or Gustavus Vassa, the African, Written By Himself.* Project Gutenberg, release date March 17, 2005, accessed December 10, 2016, http://www.gutenberg.org/files/15399/15399-h/15399-h.htm

Fisch, Audrey, ed. 2007. *The Cambridge Companion to the African American Slave Narrative*. Cambridge: Cambridge University Press.

Gates, Henry Louis Jr. 1988. *The Signifying Monkey: A Theory of African American Literary Criticism*. New York: Oxford University Press.

Gates, Henry Louis Jr. 1987. *Figures in Black: Words, Signs, and the Racial Self*. New York: Oxford University Press.

Gerzina, Gretchen Holbrook. 2001. "Mobility in Chains: Freedom of Movement in the Early Black Atlantic". *The South Atlantic Quarterly*, Vol: 100, No.1, 41—59.

Gilroy, Paul. 2002. *The Black Atlantic: Modernity and Double Consciousness*. London: Biddles Ltd.

Griffin, Farah J. 1995. *Who Set You Flowin'? The African-American Migration Narrative*. New York and Oxford: Oxford University Press.

Griffin, Farah J. and Cheryl J. Fish, eds. 1998. *A Stranger in the Village: Two Centuries of African-American Travel Writing*. Boston: Beacon Press.

Gronniosaw, James Albert Ukawsaw. 1774. *A narrative of the most remarkable particulars in the life of James Albert Ukawsaw Gronniosaw, an African Prince*. Bath Printed: Newport, Rhode-Island: Reprinted and sold by S. Southwick, in Queen Street. *Documenting the American South*. Electronic edition, 1st edition 2000, accessed December 9, 2016, http://docsouth.unc.edu/index.html

Pettinger, Alasdair, ed. 1998. *Always Elsewhere: Travels of the Black Atlantic*. London: Cassell.

Pratt, Mary Louise. 1992. *Imperial Eyes: Travel Writing and Transculturation*. London and New York: Routledge.

Smith, James McCune. 1855. "Introduction" to *Frederick Douglass. My Bondage and My Freedom*. 2003. Edited by John Stauffer. New York: Modern Library.

Stauffer, John. 2007. "Frederick Douglass's self-fashioning and the making of a Representative American man." In *The Cambridge Companion to the African American Slave Narrative*, edited by Audrey Fisch, 201—17. Cambridge: Cambridge University Press.

CHAPTER NINE

WHERE NORTH AND SOUTH MEET: MEXICO'S *NORTE* IN NORWEGIAN TRAVEL WRITING

MIEKE NEYENS

Most of the travel writers studied in this volume deal with a North of snow, mountain landscapes, dark winters and fjords. The reason for these associations is obvious: these authors "go North" in a European context. From a Mexican point of view, however, "el norte" means the desert, the US border, emigration, drug trafficking and violence. Like the North of snow and fjords, the Mexican *norte* is commonly considered a place that is utterly different from the rest of the country, and narratives (both fictional and non-fictional) of the region have in recent years been classified as a subgenre of its own, the so-called *literatura del norte* or *narcoliteratura*. The travelogue *Tequiladagbøkene* (Tequila Diaries, 2012) of the Norwegian travel writer Morten Strøksnes connects with this tendency. The desert, drug trafficking, extreme violence and illegal border crossings are important topics in the account of Strøksnes' travels in Northern Mexico. At the same time, a Norwegian traveling to Mexico is obviously "going South" and Strøksnes' text also brings a stereotyped "South" of wild nature, picturesque indigenous peoples, beautiful colonial towns; an exotic South so different from the North he comes from (and let us not forget, where his readers come from). This paper studies how *Tequiladagbøkene* connects with two traditions of writing about the Mexican *norte*: as an exotic South, and as a violent North and argues that this tension bears on the persona of the traveler.

    Tequiladagbøkene is conceived as a footstep travelogue. Strøksnes follows the route taken by another famous Norwegian, Carl Lumholtz (1851—1922), who traveled extensively in Northern Mexico in the decades around the turn of the twentieth century and published books, scientific essays and travel letters of his experiences.[1] Throughout his book, Strøksnes refers to these writings, he compares his own achievements with those of his predecessor, and compares the places he visits with Lumholtz's descriptions. According to Maria Lindgren Leavenworth (2009), footstep travelers or "second travelers" typically seek authenticity for their journeys and texts through the reference to an allegedly authentic "first traveler" and his or her writings:

> Second journeys illustrate a contemporary search for the authentic. The threat of mass tourism to destroy the possibilities of original, authentic experiences leads the second travellers to use, recycle and emphasise the first texts, which originate in a past in which authenticity is believed to be attainable. (2009, 13—14)

Retracing Lumholtz's route through northern Mexico and visiting the remote places and peoples portrayed in his works is, indeed, only one of the ways in which Strøksnes seeks to authenticate his own travels and writings. "By retracing a previously journeyed route, the second traveller thus aims to experience what the first traveller experienced and heighten the authenticity of the second journey," Leavenworth holds (Ibid., 53). A second authenticating mechanism is the emphasis of Lumholtz's qualities as an explorer in the supposedly true sense of the word. Lumholtz was driven by an adventurous spirit and scientific curiosity and made considerable efforts in order to achieve his goal to see the world: "Through risky expeditions and hard work, the social climber Lumholtz made his childhood dreams come true" (Strøksnes 2013, 7).[2] Lumholtz was humble—"he did not name anything after himself" (Ibid., 51)—and, unlike some of his Norwegian colleagues-explorers, he was not "concerned about fame or status" (Ibid., 153). He was respected by the people he met and his detailed descriptions, maps and drawings constitute an important source of knowledge, not only for scientists or amateurs of the region, but also for the indigenous populations who populate it still today (Ibid., 34, 251). Following closely in the footsteps of this great explorer into the deepest of the Sierra Madre mountains where few travelers go, Strøksnes implicitly lays claims to Lumholtz's achievements as an intrepid adventurer and discoverer of the authentic Mexico.

Thirdly and finally, Strøksnes guarantees the authenticity of his account through a sustained comparison between Lumholtz's descriptions

---

[1] Most relevant for this paper are Lumholtz (1902), (1912) and (1921).
[2] I have used the second edition of *Teauiladagbøkene* of 2013. The English translations of Strøksnes (2013) are mine.

and his own findings—a comparison that stresses how much things remain unchanged since the late nineteenth century, how much the region and its peoples still live hidden from civilization. "[Some Rarámuri women] turn demonstratively their backs upon us, as they turned their backs upon Lumholtz when he came to their country for the first time in 1891" (Ibid., 174); "Like myself, Lumholtz was surprised how healthy and strong the Rarámuri seem" (Ibid., 206); "[The Rarámuri] still live almost as they did in his [Lumholtz's] times" (Ibid., 207); "Most things look exactly as they did when Lumholtz came to [the Huichol town of] Santa Catarina" (Ibid., 289). Even when the travel writer explicitly discusses the Huichol people's contact with the world outside the Sierra Madre, he adds an anecdote which suggests precisely the lack of worldly knowledge of these "innocent" indigenous:

> The ceremonies happen as they always have done. This doesn't mean that everything stands still, or that the Huichol don't know the world outside the mountains. I sit with two elderly fellows . . . [Felipe] is almost sixty and he has hardly been away from the mountains. Two slightly fearful eyes, innocent like new snow and partly hidden under heavy, bushy eyebrows, look at me and ask how life is on the other side of the sea. How many times did I say it took to fly? . . . [Another man] is not impressed; with a worldly smile he says that Felipe and I should take the boat to Europe. "That's much cheaper than flying. And there are beds and food on board." (Ibid., 267—268)

If Lumholtz got to know the "untouched" indigenous of the Mexican Sierra Madre, so does Strøksnes, we understand.

A footstep traveler, Strøksnes thus depicts the Sierra Madre and its peoples through a "filter of the past" (Leavenworth 2009, 12), through Lumholtz's texts. Of course, the perception and description of new realities is always related to stories, images and descriptions that travelers had encountered before undertaking their journey. These existing images function as a lens or filter through which observers see the new, and they may even determine how it is experienced: "It seems a common human failing to prefer the schematic authority of a text to the disorientations of direct encounters with the human," diagnoses Edward Said ([1978] 2003, 93). If this "textual attitude" is present in all travel experiences and writings, albeit unconsciously most often, it marks footstep travel explicitly. Footstep travelers are forced to negotiate their textual attitude towards the reality they encounter on their trip. The filter of the first travel texts, Leavenworth asserts (2009, 53), may function as a "liberation" for the footstep travelers, when "textual elements define and justify the second journey text"; or it may, in turn, limit the experiences of the second traveler, "resulting in the present having to be ignored in favour of the past the second traveller has come to see." With only Strøksnes' text at hand, it is impossible to determine to what degree Lumholtz's writings determined the footstep traveler's perceptions and experiences in Mexico. However, we will see that the chapters of *Tequiladagbøkene* that deal with Lumholtz's route privilege an exoticized image of a "wild" and "uncivilized" Mexico where the traveler can go native and discover his primitive Self, while the passages of other places bring a modern Mexico where violence and chaos rule and where the traveler is forced to negotiate the traditional persona of the fearless, heroic adventurer.

Going South in exotic Mexico

Tequiladagbøkene contains all the necessary ingredients of the prototypical modern travel book as defined by scholars like Carl Thompson (2011) and Tim Youngs (2013). It features an individual traveler searching to get away from everyday life, longing for adventure and freedom, for a simple life. "The desert makes me want to live in a tent and not own anything, except for my own freedom," Strøksnes writes for example at an early point of his trip (2013, 20). In Mexico, we read, he seeks to get away from civilization and experience "rare places that one wouldn't reach without a certain effort" (120). For Strøksnes, physical challenge is a necessary ingredient of so-called real travel. He repeatedly describes his suffering and endurance, his seemingly heroic exploits and explicitly distances himself from common, "lazy" tourists. His overcoming of the difficulties encountered *en route* grants him credit and authority (Youngs 2013, 87).

Strøksnes often focuses on all that appears unfamiliar and overwhelming to him as a Norwegian; as foreign travel writers in Mexico have done for centuries, and as they have done for many other places as well. Taking into account the broader context of travel writing of Mexico, Strøksnes is thus not only following in the footsteps of Lumholtz, he recycles many of the stereotypes spread in travelogues of Mexico (and of Latin America, more in general) and studied by scholars as Mary Louise Pratt ([1992] 2008), Daniel Cooper Alarcón (1997), Thea Pitman (2008), Carlos Monsiváis (1984), and many others. I will here highlight three of these topoï that we find in Strøksnes' account of Mexico as an exotic South.

A first feature of this exotic Mexico in *Tequiladagbøkene* is the representation of the country as "magical" or unreal. Throughout the book, northern Mexico is described as a place that is not entirely real, that is somehow located on the border of reality as we know it. In Mexico, mystery rules, there are secrets everywhere. In Mexico, Strøksnes claims when attending a local wrestling match, "the borders between fiction and reality overlap" (Strøksnes 2013, 221). Other examples include the description of the Pinacate desert as a "strange planet" (Ibid., 48) and the desert town of Real de Catorce as "a world full of secrets," where "something special hangs in the air" (Ibid., 240). On his way to the Pacific, Strøksnes tells of his stopovers in "small mountain towns with a strange, dark atmosphere, where people hardly talk or make eye contact with strangers . . . people sit in their houses like shadows" (Ibid., 215). In the following passage, he explicitly describes the Mexican landscape as seemingly unreal, as a "drawing" or a "postcard":

> The view of [the river] Rio Chapalagano [sic] a couple of thousand meter under us appears more as a drawing than as reality. Towards the top of the mountains on the other side, we can distinguish [the town of] Santa Catarina. In the sunset the mountains glow deep pink. A warm wind presses up from the depths of the gorge alongside the mountainsides. Together with the darkness rises a blood red moon from behind those same mountains. It is like a postcard in full size. (Ibid., 282)

We get a similar description from the bus that takes the traveler through the Chihuahua desert. Here, the landscape looks like a "barnebok" (children's book) with "unaturlige farger" (unnatural colors) (Ibid., 159—160).

Closely related to the representation of Mexico as a borderland between the real and the unreal is the alleged "mythical" status of the Sierra Madre mountains in the country's North-West. Like Lumholtz, Strøksnes attributes the qualifier "mythical" to the Sierra Madre mountain chain. From the Arizona desert where he starts his journey he writes: "If everything goes as planned, I will reach Mexico City in two months, after traveling through this borderland and the wild and mythical Sierra Madre mountains" (Ibid., 19). The Mythical Sierra Madre is an image repeated on the book's back cover and on the publisher's website. Why the mountain chain is said to be mythical or what this adjective actually refers to is, however, never explained.

All in all, northern Mexico is described as a liminal space where the real world meets a fictitious one. In this borderland the traveler puts his masculinity to test and does not cringe from bending the local laws in order to satisfy his search for authenticity—what is allowed and what not seems to be flexible when one is far away from "civilization". Thus Strøksnes narrates how his obsession with the inaccessible holy places of the indigenous Tohono and Huichol leads him to visit these sites without authorization, take as many notes and pictures as he can and then hurry away. The goals the traveler has set himself seem to be more demanding than the respect for local Huichol authorities. "We have some kind of 'authorization' to go to [the holy valley] Teakáta," he writes, "how solid this authorization really is, I don't ask. [Like my travel companion] I am becoming restless myself, and we cannot sit here and wait all night [for the authorization]" (Ibid., 293). Later he qualifies his visit of Teakáta as "unauthorized" and describes how he had to run from Huichol police (Ibid., 307). Still, "for once, I am satisfied with everything" (Ibid., 307).

A second feature of *Tequiladagbøkene*'s exotic Mexico is that of a country of pure nature. Mary Louise Pratt has influentially analyzed Alexander von Humboldt's writings and those of the many travelers-capitalists Humboldt inspired to go and explore Latin America in the name of science—yet most often representing a project of neocolonial imperialism and expansion. According to Pratt, these nineteenth-century travel writers reduced the continent to "pure nature" (2008, 123). In the Victorian tradition of the late nineteenth and early twentieth century, landscape depictions abandon the scientific discourse to the benefit of an estheticizing one: landscapes are described as paintings meant to please the reader. Still, Pratt argues, a logic of power and dominion pervades these verbal paintings: Victorian travelers authorize themselves to describe the view from their vantage point, as well as to evaluate and thus in a way possess what they see (Ibid., 200—201).

While the Victorian travel writings presented, according to Pratt, a "density of meaning . . . achieved especially through a huge number of adjectival modifiers" (Ibid., 200), *Tequiladagbøkene* includes relatively straightforward landscape descriptions. They mostly consist of short sentences and use adjectives related to the basic colors and the traveler's perception of outdoor temperature (warm, cool, cold); metaphors are rare, and the verbal constructions often are *to be, to have, there is/there are.* Nonetheless, Strøksnes' account does confirm and reinforce the longstanding conception of Mexico as a country of natural abundance, of wild and pure nature, and it offers landscape descriptions as verbal tableaux, often seen from a mountain top, as in the passage of the Río Chapalagana quoted above, as well as in the following example:

> The sun is about to come up. In a couple of hours the world will have soft colors. The river Casas Grandes calmly trickles by, some hundred meter further on. Along the riversides there are big green broadleaf trees. The branches vibrate with hyperactive little birds, and the tweeting is the only sound that breaks the silence. The air is cool and clear. (Ibid., 120)

A third and final element of *Tequiladagbøkene*'s exoticizing discourse of Mexico relates to the representation of the indigenous of the Sierra Madre. As mentioned, Strøksnes privileges an image of the Huichol and Rarámuri as traditional, unworldly peoples living cut off from civilization. In addition, he reproduces the longstanding stereotype of the mysterious indigenous. When he is about to start hiking his way into the deepest of the Sierra Madre, Strøksnes considers what he expects to find there:

> In these mountains there are many isolated, shy and secretive Indian peoples with very distinctive ancient cultures. . . . There are still some hundred indigenous peoples in Mexico, and many of them still live in a traditional way. But few do so to the extent of indigenous peoples in the heart of the Sierra Madre. (Ibid., 169)

As readers we are therefore perhaps little surprised when some pages further on we find the following description of the traveler's actual first meeting with the Rarámuri people of the Sierra Madre:

> We [Strøksnes and his guide] go past a river. Some Rarámuri women in traditional colorful clothes are crossing over. As soon as they become aware of our presence, they turn their backs on us ostentatiously. (Ibid., 174)

The traveler found what he knew he would find. He then goes on to briefly sketch the history of Rarámuri shyness and concludes: "The Rarámuri, who were and are extremely shy, also among each other, learned that it was best to avoid contact, or to have it on their own terms as often as possible" (Ibid., 175).

The image of the silent, mysterious indigenous peoples of Mexico has a history that goes back to colonial texts and became widely spread through the writings of the already mentioned Alexander von Humboldt and Carl Lumholtz. In the *Tequiladagbøkene,* the cliché is repeated throughout the book. Here is another example of Strøksnes meeting Rarámuri—strikingly similar to the previous one:

> It is in one of these narrow ravines that we for the first time meet Rarámuri from nearby. We see the two men deep down in the valley, but they move upwards at high speed. They both have colorful wide shirts, short dresses, around the upper-body, thin headbands and self-made sandals. We step aside on the narrow path while they swiftly jog past us, without saying a word or showing that they had noted our presence in any way. (Ibid., 186)

Besides "mysterious", "traditional" and "colorful", we learn, among other things, that the Rarámuri are less reserved when they have had some alcohol (Ibid., 208), that they are "a peaceful people," except when they are drunken (Ibid.). Many of the same assertions are made with regard to another indigenous group Strøksnes meets in the Sierra Madre, the Huichol people. They too are repeatedly described as "colorful" (Ibid., 250, 267) and reserved: "People overlook us in a passive-friendly way," (Ibid., 267); "No one looks at me," (Ibid., 270); "the women turn their backs as soon as they see us, as if we were unclean," (Ibid., 289). They too seem to have a difficult relation to alcohol (Ibid., 262, 311).

All in all, the indigenous in their strangeness and otherness are a central element of *Tequiladagbøkene*'s discourse on Mexico, northern Mexico in particular—as they are and have been in many travelogues of the region. Despite being very conscious of the workings of the travel writing genre and discussing some of its unfortunate mechanisms and effects, Strøksnes does not seem to be able to avoid its pitfalls. Indeed, while he writes of the Tohono people that "they were neither belligerent nor picturesque enough" (Ibid., 21) to be interesting for Europeans, Strøksnes himself seems to find indigenous people interesting in as far as they are exotically and traditionally living deep down in the mountains where little has changed since Lumholtz visited the area. And while he programmatically states that a travel writer should call indigenous people the way they want to be called and therefore employs the term *Rarámuri* instead of *Tarahumara* "as all the others do" (Ibid., 170), Strøksnes makes use of ethnic labels such as "Indians", "mestizos", "ethnic Mexicans" uncritically, without ever discussing them. Finally, while he criticizes how US enthusiasts hyped the Rarámuri running culture and made big money out of films, books and gadgets without the Rarámuri themselves sharing in it (Ibid., 178), there is no discussion in the book of the responsibility Strøksnes sees for himself in this matter—except maybe for the mention in passing of the money he pays to his young Huichol guide: "The tip I put in his pocket . . . is big enough for him to go to school. He will give it to his father right away. Let us hope the latter doesn't drink it" (Ibid., 310—311). The travel writer seems to be trapped in the logic of the genre he denounces.

To sum up, *Tequiladagbøkene* presents Mexico and the Sierra Madre as a mysterious place of beautiful nature and colorful indigenous peoples. It presents Mexico as utterly different from all the traveler and his readers are familiar with, as an exotic South, the exotic South as it is experienced by a traveler from the European North and as it has been experienced by many of his colleagues before him. Yet, as mentioned in the introduction, the region that Strøksnes depicts lies, from a central Mexican point of view, obviously in the North, "el norte."

Going North in cruel Mexico

A borderland, Northern Mexico has traditionally been associated with bandits and smugglers, rebels, outcasts and minor criminals; just think of the charming revolutionary leader Francisco "Pancho" Villa. Nowadays, stories of *el norte*—be it newspaper items, travelogues, reportages or novels—tend to focus on the major criminal network of drug trafficking and how its perverse logics affect all levels of daily life in the area. *El norte* is different from the rest of the country, and, as mentioned, in recent years publishers and scholars have started to consider narratives about the region as a genre of its own. *Tequiladagbøkene* connects with both the discourse of *el norte* and this relatively new vogue of writing about Northern Mexico.

Firstly, there is obviously the omnipresence of drug-related violence in the *literatura norteña* (Parra 2004; Palaversich 2007; Fuentes Kraffczyk 2012), and the related themes of danger and fear, corruption and chaos. Strøksnes' account of his stay in the northern Mexican city of Ciudad Juárez is one long description of how narco-violence has turned Juárez into a dead city—a city where death literally is everywhere and where public life is dead. "Welcome in the world-capital of murder," he begins his account of the city, and continues:

> Every week, tortured, decapitated, mutilated bodies are dumped across the city. On top of that, hundreds of people have disappeared, and those left behind have no idea of what might have happened. No one knows for sure how many get kidnapped, because this kind of crimes are rarely reported to the police. What everybody knows, however, is that the police often is involved. Ciudad Juárez has become a city of bizarre rumors, morbid codes, of fear and death. (Ibid., 75)

This is one of many examples of violent, fear-struck northern Mexico as it is depicted in *Tequiladagbøkene*.

Secondly, like many *narconovelas* (Fonseca 2009, 9), Strøksnes' account of the harsh realities of *el norte*, favors the viewpoint of artists and intellectuals. His main interlocutors on this part of the trip are a university professor and poet, recognized journalists, a news photographer and a priest. All of them fight the drug cartels in their own way. The poet-professor Javier Sicilia, for instance, organizes peace rallies in several of the cities on the traveler's route. Strøksnes dedicates a whole chapter to Sicilia, whose son was murdered by narco-criminals. Tirelessly, Sicilia fights the drug cartels, the political elites, the mafias, the army: "Sicilia doesn't look tired. He is an obstinate man struck with grief who tries to create something meaningful out of his son's death" (Ibid., 238). Strøksnes' contacts in narco-Mexico are depicted as modest heroes, trying to make a difference in a perverse reality.

Thirdly, the *literatura norteña* frequently includes landscape depictions, particularly desert landscapes, and references to the harsh climate (Parra 2004). So does *Tequiladagbøkene*. Whereas the exotic Northern Mexico of picturesque Indians is associated with mountains, canyons and lush nature, the violent *norte* of ruthless drug cartels is associated with desert and unbearable heat. In the company of the desert-enthusiast Richard Laugharn, Strøksnes climbs to the top of the Sierra Guterrada in the Pinacata desert:

> It is too hot to stick around and enjoy the view. So we climb down and start to walk back [to the car] over the sand dunes. . . . My head aches and I feel dizzy. The last bottle of water is now half, and I would have liked to drink it down in one gulp, for my tongue feels like a piece of wood. It is well over 40 degrees now. I no longer know where the car is, whether I might have gone too much to the left or the right. (Ibid., 53)

Fourthly and finally, the Mexican literature of the North frequently employs the metaphor of the degenerating body, symbolizing the degenerating Mexican society (Fuentes Kraffczyk 2012). The image of physical degeneration is also repeated in Strøksnes' account of the Mexican *norte*. The above-mentioned passage of the hiking trip into the Pinacate desert results in a detailed description not only of the concrete effects of the excruciating heat on the traveler's own body (dizziness, headache, fever), but also of all the internal physical processes that affect a person dying of thirst—first convulsions, loss of conscience and hallucinations, before the last phase sets in:

> The blood hardly circulates through the veins anymore. It is more like sticky, red mud. All organs receive too little liquid and oxygen. . . . One turns really red, the skin becomes extremely sensitive and the slightest touch hurts. Perhaps that is why one takes off all clothes and runs around laughing like a madman and hallucinating. . . . The muscles have start to eat themselves now. It means that they are rotting. Chunks of damaged tissue start to block the central organs like kidneys, bladder and heart. . . . The organs fall out. Then it is finally over. (Ibid., 55—56)

Also the violent city of Juárez affects the traveler physically. While having dinner with his journalist friend, for example, he comments on the impact the city has on his body: "What should have been a relaxing, social evening, has become a catalogue of the misery in the city. I begin to feel exhausted, or rather satiated" (Ibid., 105). In another passage, he qualifies the Mexican drug mafia as a "cannibalistic organization" (Ibid., 94). Finally, when leaving Juárez, Strøksnes concludes that it is "an overdose of a city" (Ibid., 116).

An area of tremendous heat, excessive violence and bodily degeneration, the severe North has an impact on the self-presentation of the traveler. While he in the "exotic south" highlighted his heroic achievements despite the many dangers and challenges on the trip, he seems to accept the limits of his physical strength in the "harsh north". In the desert, he bumps into a cactus and depends on his guide to remove the many spines—"I felt like a puppy," he declares (Ibid., 47). In the murder city of Ciudad Juarez, reality forces the traveler to readjust his expectations and literary ambitions:

> I had planned to write of how the city, despite everything, actually functions. Of how common people strive and live. Ciudad Juárez by day. Thereafter I would do research on all the bad things and continue to write under the working title Ciudad Juárez by night. . . . [My local guide Miguel disapproves:] If I am looking for something nice and functioning, I should have gone somewhere else. The city is in hands of killers, suffering from a total crisis on all levels, both by day and night. (Ibid., 80—81)

Unlike the passages of the Sierra Madre, in Ciudad Juárez there is no room for hero-like adventures. Struck by fear, the traveler keeps to the safety of his hotel and accepts his weakness:

> I do as everybody else in the ghost city of Juárez, where people hide themselves behind walls and fences, where the sound of gunfire wakes sleeping babies, and where no one opens the door when it is knocked upon. Like this I sit and become a part of Juárez. (Ibid., 91—92)

> I feel that I should try to experience some of the things that go on in the city. This is my only chance, Ciudad Juárez is hardly a city I will visit again. So I go to a kind of club I noticed earlier on, just across the street from my hotel. The club is surrounded by soldiers with heavy automatic weapons, but inside there are only two other guests . . . I think it is just not worth it, turn around and cross the street to the hotel. Me too, I am struck by fear. (Ibid., 105—106)

Tequiladagbøkene thus represents Northern Mexico both as part of a large exotic South and as a violent *norte*. My analysis has shown that the book connects with two literary traditions of writing about the region: European travel writing (and Norwegian exploration writing in particular) and the so-called *narcoliteratura*. These discourses construct *el norte* as utterly different, as a strange place with its own natural environment and social rules and regulations. However, whereas exotic Mexico offers the traveler the opportunity to stage himself as a heroic explorer, the many dangers of harsh Mexico oblige him to represent himself as vulnerable and sensible. In this way, harsh Mexico opens for innovative travel writing.

References

Cooper Alarcón, Daniel. 1997. *The Aztec Palimpsest: Mexico in the Modern Imagination*. Tucson: University of Arizona Press.

Fonseca, Alberto. 2009. *Cuando llovió dinero en Macondo: literatura y narcotráfico en Colombia y México,* unpublished Phd thesis, University of Kansas.

Fuentes Kraffzyk, Felipe Oliver. 2012. "'Narconovela' mexicana. ¿Moda o subgénero?" *Taller de letras*. Vol: 50, 105—21.

Leavenworth, Maria Lindgren. 2010. *The Second Journey. Travelling in Literary Footsteps*. Umeå: Institutionen för språkstudier.

Lumholtz, Carl. 2011 [1902]. *Unknown Mexico: A Record of Five Years' Exploration among Tribes of the Western Sierra Madre, in the Tierra Caliente of Tepic and Jalisco; and among the Tarascos of Michoacan*. 2 vols. New York: Scribner.

—. 1912. *New Trails in Mexico: An Account of One Year's Exploration in North-western Sonora, Mexico, and South-western Arizona, 1909–1910*. London: T. Fisher Unwin.

—. 1921. "My Life of Exploration". *Natural History* Vol: 21, No. 3, 224—43.

Monsiváis, Carlos. 1984. "Travelers in Mexico: A Brief Anthology of Selected Myths". *Diogenes*. Vol: 32, 48—74.

Palaversich, Diana. 2007. "La nueva narrativa del norte: moviendo fronteras de la literatura mexicana". *Symposium: A Quarterlly Journal in Modern Literatures*. Vol: 61, No. 1, 9—26.

Parra, Eduardo Antonio. 2004. "El lenguaje de la narrativa del norte de México". *Revista de crítica literaria latinoamericana*. Vol: 59, 71—7.

Pitman, Thea. 2008. *Mexican Travel Writing*. Oxford: Peter Lang.

Pratt, Mary Louise. 2008 [1992]. *Imperial Eyes: Travel Writing and Transculturation*. London: Routledge.

Said, Edward W. 2003 [1978]. *Orientalism*. London: Penguin.

Strøksnes, Morten. 2013 [2012]. *Tequiladagbøkene: Gjennom Sierra Madre*. Oslo: Kagge.

Thompson, Carl. 2011. *Travel Writing*. London: Routledge.

Youngs, Tim. 2013. *The Cambridge Introduction to Travel Writing*. Cambridge: Cambridge University Press.

CONTRIBUTORS

Eva Lambertsson Björk (dr) teaches Intercultural Communication at various levels, including a Master's programme in English for language teachers at Østfold University College, Halden, Norway. Her academic background is in English literature and English for specific purposes. She served as the Dean of her faculty from 1996 to 2009. Since 2010, her academic work has included close cooperation with Dr Jutta Eschenbach at Østfold University College. This cooperation has led to, among other projects, the development of a teaching method based on film fragments, *Reel Life*, for which they were awarded Østfold University College's award for innovative teaching in 2013. Current research interests include, in addition to travel literature, intercultural learning and issues related to identity construction. **eva.l.bjork@hiof.no**

Jutta Eschenbach (dr) teaches Intercultural Communication at various levels, including a Master's programme in German for language teachers at Østfold University College, Halden, Norway. Her background includes, among other academic fields, German for specific purposes and intercultural studies. Since 2010 her academic work has been done in close cooperation with Dr Eva Lambertsson Björk at Østfold University College. This cooperation has led to, among other projects, the development of a teaching method based on film fragments, *Reel Life*, for which they were awarded Østfold University College's award for innovative teaching in 2013. Current research interests include, in addition to travel literature, intercultural learning and issues related to identity construction. **jutta.eschenbach@hiof.no**

Oana Cogenau (dr) teaches English literature, cultural studies and translation studies at Alexandru Ioan Cuza University of Iaşi, Romania. She has authored an *Introduction to African-American Travel Literature* (2013); edited volumes in cultural studies (*Wounded Bodies, Wounded Minds*, 2014) and on intercultural issues (*Travel and Intercultural Communication in Europe*, 2016); and published articles on a range of authors and topics, with a special interest in African-American literature and a constant focus on travel. She has given lectures in travel and translation studies at universities in several European countries and taught Romanian language, culture and civilisation in South Korea. **oa_na_co@yahoo.com**

Melanie Duckworth (dr) teaches British and Postcolonial Literature at Østfold University College, Halden, Norway. Her publications include "Grievous Music: Randolph Stow's Middle Ages" (*Australian Literary Studies*, 2011), "Les Murray and Australian Poetry: Time, Place and Belonging" (*Bøygen*, 2012), and "This is a true book: Australian national myths, childhood and storytelling in Randolph Stow's *Midnite: The Story of a Wild Colonial Boy* (1967) and *The Merry-go-round in the Sea* (1965)" (*Narratology Plus: Studies in Recent International Narratives for Children and Young Adults,* forthcoming*)*. Her current research interests include contemporary poetry and the environment, temporality, and animals. **melanie.duckworth@hiof.no**

Janicke Stensvaag Kaasa has a PhD in Comparative Literature from the University of Oslo, Norway. She recently defended her doctoral thesis, entitled *Shaped by the North, shaping the North: English-Canadian Travel Writing in the 1950s*, on the representation of the Canadian North in a selection of English-Canadian travel books. She currently holds a completion grant at the University of Oslo. **j.s.kaasa@ilos.uio.no**

Karen Patrick Knutsen is Professor of English literature and TESOL at Østfold University College in Halden, Norway. She specializes in contemporary English literature and has also worked within children's and young adult literature in connection with teacher education. She is the author of *Reciprocal Haunting: Pat Barker's Regeneration Trilogy* (Waxmann, 2010) and has co-edited a number of anthologies: *Modi Operandi: Perspektiver på kriminallitteratur* (Høgskolen i Østfold, 2003); *Genre and Cultural Competence: An Interdisciplinary Approach to the Study of Text* (Waxmann, 2010); and *Narratives of Risk: Interdisciplinary Studies* (Waxmann, 2012). At present she is co-editing the anthology *Narratology Plus: Studies in Recent International Narratives for Children and Young Adults*, forthcoming at Peter Lang Verlag. **karen.p.knutsen@hiof.no**

Mieke Neyens holds a PhD in Hispanic Studies from the University of Oslo, Norway. Her research focuses on Latin American travel writing, Spanish literature and Spanish didactics. She has published in international journals such as *Travel Writing Studies* (Routledge) and *Bulletin of*

Hispanic Studies (Liverpool). She currently teaches Spanish language and culture at Centrum voor Levende Talen (KU Leuven).
mieke.neyens@yahoo.com

Maria Selezneva is a third year PhD student at the University of Exeter (England) in the Department of Modern Languages. In her research she explores translation in the field of travel and tourism. In 2012 Maria graduated from Chelyabinsk State University where she studied Linguistics and Translation for 5 years. Maria's theoretical side of the research is supported by her practical experience in freelance translation.
ms571@exeter.ac.uk

Kathryn Walchester (dr) teaches in the Department of English and Cultural History at Liverpool John Moores University, UK. Her research interests are alternative modes of Grand Tour and Home Tour travel in the eighteenth and nineteenth century and travel in and to the North. Her publications include *'Our Own Fair Italy'; Nineteenth-Century Women's Travel Writing and Italy 1800-1844* (Peter Lang, 2007), *Gamle Norge; Nineteenth-Century British Women Travellers and Norway* (Anthem, 2014) and *Travel Writing: 100 Keywords* (Anthem, in press 2017), co-edited with Zoe Kinsley and Charles Forsdick. She is currently working on a monograph about working and travelling, *Servants and the British Travelogue 1750-1850.* **k.m.walchester@ljmu.ac.uk**

Joanna Witkowska is a lecturer at the University of Szczecin, Faculty of Languages, Poland. Her research focuses on Polish-British cultural relationships. She has published on anti-Western propaganda and Polish-British relations during WWII. Her publications include *The Image of The United Kingdom in Poland During the Stalinist Period* (Wydawnictwo Naukowe Uniwersytetu Szczecińskiego, Szczecin 2009) and "The Polish Army in Exile: Cultural Constructions and Reconstructions of the British Other" in: Joanna Witkowska, Uwe Zagratzki, eds. *Exile and Migration. Reflections on an Old Practise* (Verlag Dr. Kovac, Hamburg 2016).
joannawitkowska1@poczta.onet.pl